CW00689903

The operation of transm scanning electron micro

Dawn Chescoe
Micro Structural Studies Unit,
University of Surrey

and

Peter J. Goodhew
Department of Materials Science and Engineering,
University of Liverpool

Oxford University Press · Royal Microscopical Society · 1990

Oxford University Press, Walton Street, Oxford OX2 6DP

Oxford New York Toronto
Delhi Bombay Calcutta Madras Karachi
Petaling Jaya Singapore Hong Kong Tokyo
Nairobi Dar es Salaam Cape Town
Melbourne Auckland

and associated companies in
Berlin Ibadan

Royal Microscopical Society
37/38 St. Clements
Oxford OX4 1AJ

Oxford is a trade mark of Oxford University Press

Published in the United States
by Oxford University Press, New York

British Library Cataloguing in Publication Data
Chescoe, Dawn
The operation of transmission and scanning electron
microscopes.
1. Electron microscopes
I. Title   II. Goodhew, Peter J. (Peter John) 1943–
502.825
ISBN 0–19–856420–1 (pbk)

Library of Congress Cataloging in Publication Data
Chescoe, Dawn.
The operation of transmission and scanning electron microscopes
Dawn Chescoe and Peter J. Goodhew.
p.   cm.—(Microscopy handbooks; 20)
Includes bibliographical references.
1. Scanning electron microscopes—Technique.   2. Transmission
electron microscopes—Technique.   I. Goodhew, Peter J.   II. Royal
Microscopical Society (Great Britain).   III. Title.   IV. Series.
[DNLM: 1. Microscopy, Electron, Scanning—methods.   QH 212.S3
C524o]
QH212.S3C44   1990   578'.45—dc20   89–72167
ISBN 0–19–856420–1 (pbk.)

Typeset by Cotswold Typesetting Ltd, Cheltenham
Printed in Great Britain by Bookcraft, Midsomer Norton, Avon

Preface

The aim of this booklet is to explain the essential operations which lead to the taking of useful micrographs with modern scanning and transmission electron microscopes. We have attempted at all stages to relate the turning of knobs to what is going on in the microscope, since it is only by *understanding* the alignment and operating procedures that an appreciation of the potential and limitations of the instruments can be developed. At the same time we have tried to eliminate material which the user either does not need to know or which is peculiar to a particular type of application or specimen. Thus we have not attempted to discuss field emission guns, which are found on very few instruments, nor have we described in detail any contrast mechanisms, a knowledge of which will enable microscope users to interpret their micrographs. Our limited objective in such a few pages is to enable the reader to take the first few hundred successful micrographs and to put him or her in a position from which to develop into a skilled and knowledgeable microscopist.

Guildford   D.C.
1989   P.J.G.

Contents

1 How and why electron microscopes work

The history of electron microscopy stretches back about fifty years. A major driving force for the development of all types of electron microscope (EM) has been the desire to overcome some of the limitations of the light microscope. It would seem that, using electrons with wavelengths much less than 0.1 nm (1 Å), the resolution of the light microscope (which is limited by visible wavelengths to about half a micrometre) could be greatly improved. This has proved to be the case. In addition, the depth of field and depth of focus of electron microscopes has proved to be much better than those of a light microscope at the same magnification.

For these reasons, together with the simultaneous potential for analysis which modern electron microscopes provide, two types of EM have been developed very rapidly. We now classify EMs into two major groups: scanning electron microscopes (SEMs) which are mainly used to study surface morphology and transmission electron microscopes (TEMs) which enable us to explore the internal structure of a thin specimen.

Many of the components of different EMs are very similar. This introductory chapter therefore contains sections which apply to all types of EM and those which describe the operation of the SEM and the TEM separately. The main interest of each reader is likely to lie initially with one of these types (although we hope that you will eventually develop an appreciation of the full range). Readers whose primary interest lies in SEM are recommended to omit Sections 1.2, 1.9, and 1.10 at a first reading, while those who wish to learn about the TEM should omit Sections 1.1, 1.7, and 1.8.

1.1. The scanning electron microscope

The principle of operation of a scanning electron microscope (SEM) is very simple and can be understood by referring to Fig. 1. A fine beam of electrons (B) is scanned across the surface of the specimen in synchronism with the spot of the display cathode ray tube (CRT). A detector monitors the intensity of a chosen secondary signal from the specimen (for example secondary electrons) and the brightness of the CRT spot is controlled by an amplified version of the detected signal. If, for any reason, the intensity of the emitted secondary signal changes across the specimen then contrast will be seen in the image on the CRT.

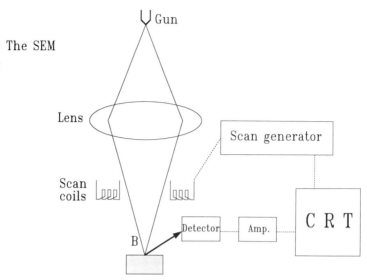

Fig. 1. The components of a scanning electron microscope. CRT = cathode ray tube display.

It is fortunate that, as it is most commonly used, an SEM produces images which are readily interpreted because they contain light and shade in much the same way as everyday images which are familiar to our eye. Thus holes appear dark and hills have a bright side and a shadowed side. It is important to realize, however, that the way in which the image is formed may be radically different from the way in which the human eye collects an image. One obvious difference is that there is no 'ray path' between the object and the image screen and this accounts for the importance of electronics in manipulating and displaying the image before it is displayed on a cathode ray tube. A second significant difference is that the eye is sensitive to all points of an image simultaneously (the image points are received 'in parallel') while an SEM image is collected point by point, that is, in 'serial' fashion.

A further important consideration is that the image formed in an SEM is not necessarily of the surface. It is possible, by choosing the electron energy, to control the depth to which the electrons penetrate and the type of emitted signal used to form the image. This gives the microscopist a great deal of control over the nature of the final image. However, it also means that the microscopist needs to understand how the image is formed before being able to interpret it sensibly. This slim manual does not attempt to deal seriously with this topic and for this reason we recommended that you study a textbook such as Goodhew and Humphreys (1988) as well.

Many different types of image can be formed in an SEM depending on the nature of the secondary signal which is chosen for detection. The common types of detector, and hence the easily-available image modes, are discussed in Section 1.8. Analysis, using the emitted X-ray signal, is a very important extension of modern SEM but it requires very little alignment and is not dealt with here.

The major components of the SEM which require careful alignment and need to be set up properly are the electron gun, the condenser lens(es) which form the illumination system and generate the fine beam, the scan coils, and the detector. All these components are shown in Fig. 1. Their operation as individual components is described in detail in Sections 1.3 to 1.6 and the way in which they are assembled into a working SEM is treated in Section 1.7. All SEMs also contain small apertures which limit the angular spread of the electron beam and the positioning and alignment of these are considered in Section 1.7 and Chapter 3.

1.2. The transmission electron microscope

Before we can consider the details of how a transmission electron micro-scope (TEM) works we must be clear as to why it works at all. It is not at all obvious that passing a beam of electrons through a thin specimen should enable us to see anything within it. Let us consider very briefly the possible interactions between the electrons of the beam and the atoms of the solid specimen. Each electron passing through the specimen has a number of possible fates. The most significant of these are:

(a) It is undeflected (i.e. transmitted without interacting with any atom).

(b) It is deflected but loses no energy (i.e. elastically scattered).

(c) It loses a significant amount of energy and is probably deflected (i.e. inelastically scattered). As a result secondary electrons or X-rays may be excited.

If all these types of electrons (we will call them a, b, and c) are allowed to carry on down the microscope they will all contribute to the image and all regions of the specimen will look the same. There would be no *contrast* between areas of different thickness or different composition. In order to create *contrast* in the image we must separate the scattered electrons (b and/or c) from the unscattered electrons (a) using the objective lens aper-ture (see Sections 1.5 and 3.5).

Figure 2 illustrates schematically the fate of each 100 electrons falling on a (rather unusual!) model specimen. Region (a) consists of 10 nm of amor-phous carbon, which is a light atom. This scatters electrons very weakly and only 9 of the 100 electrons will be deflected by 0.5° or more. None are likely to be deflected by more than a few degrees. Region (b) is an area of twice the thickness and scatters slightly more strongly: 17 electrons are significantly deflected. Region (c) is the same thickness as (b) but consists of amorphous lead (a very heavy atom); here the majority of electrons are

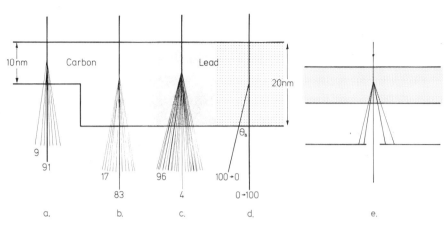

Fig. 2. The fate of 100 electrons falling on four different regions of a hypothetical specimen. The numbers shown are those scattered through more than 0.5° and those unscattered. The regions are as follows: (a) 10 nm of amorphous carbon; (b) 20 nm of amorphous carbon; (c) 20 nm of amorphous lead and (d) 20 nm of crystalline lead; (e) shows the effect of inserting an objective aperture to stop all electrons scattered through more than about 0.5°.

deflected but still only through a small angle. Region (d) consists of the same thickness of crystalline lead. In this region diffraction can take place and the scattered electron beam will be reinforced in certain directions but cancelled in others, resulting in most of the scattered electrons travelling in specific directions at twice the Bragg angle θ_B, to the unscattered beam. The number of electrons emerging from the specimen in the unscattered and diffracted beams depends critically on the specimen orientation and thickness and may be anything from almost zero to 100 in each case.

If all 100 electrons are allowed to travel down the microscope the 'image' produced by the lenses will show no difference between regions (a), (b), (c). and (d)—there will be no contrast. If, however, we can arrange to stop all those electrons which have been scattered through more than 0.5°, by inserting an aperture below the specimen as shown in Fig. 2(e), then regions (a)–(d) will look quite different. The brightness of the image of each region will be proportional to the number of unscattered electrons which pass through the aperture, so regions (a), (b), and (c) will appear to have brightness in the ratio 91:83:4. The lead will thus be clearly visible as a dark region, whereas thickness variations in the carbon regions will give only faint contrast.

In practice the aperture is inserted in the microscope column at the back focal plane of the objective lens, as will appear in Section 1.9 below. Although this objective aperture does not appear to feature prominently in the following description of the operation and alignment of a microscope, it should be borne in mind that it holds the key to forming any *useful* image in a transmission microscope.

The optics of the instrument are now described and the way in which each of the components works is explained. The electron microscope is closely analogous to a projection light microscope used in transmission and both have the following major components (Fig. 3): there must be a source of illumination, a condenser system to collimate the illumination on to the specimen, an objective lens to provide a first focused image, a projector system to magnify this image to its final size, a screen on which to view the image and finally a camera with which to record it. Since all the lenses work in much the same way, and the screen and camera are extremely simple we really only have two components to discuss; the electron gun and the typical electromagnetic lens. We shall see later that there are a few other components in a real electron microscope but let us start with the fundamental two, which are common to both scanning and transmission microscopes.

1.3. The thermionic electron gun

The vast majority of electron microscopes use a thermionic triode electron

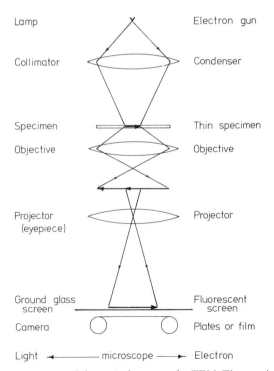

Fig. 3. The major components of the optical system of a TEM. The terminology in common use in light microscopy is indicated on the left. The equivalent terms in electron microscopy are shown on the right.

gun. This serves not only as a source of accelerated electrons but as a pre-liminary 'condenser lens'. It therefore produces an intense beam of high energy electrons which is directed down the microscope column. This of course is more than is usually obtained from the 'light bulb' source of illumination in a light microscope, which tends to be omnidirectional.

The structure of a thermionic electron gun is shown diagrammatically in Fig. 4. A filament is heated to white heat and gives off many thermionic electrons. These are accelerated towards an anode and pass through a hole in its centre to the condenser system of the microscope. Application of a 'bias' to the Wehnelt cap causes the gun to act like a triode valve and as an electrostatic lens. The electrons are thus only emitted from a limited region of the filament and their trajectories cross over on their way to the anode hole. Looking from below (i.e. from the point of view of the microscope) all the electrons appear to come from the cross-over point (C), which is there-fore often called the 'virtual source'. One of the most useful features of this gun is that it not only accelerates a beam of electrons but it makes them appear to diverge from a source which is only some micrometres across although they really come from a region on the filament which is some hundreds of micrometres in extent.

There are three parameters which we can control in our operation of this gun. These are the filament current (and hence temperature), the grid bias, and the accelerating voltage (or 'high tension'). These will be examined in turn to establish the criteria for setting them. The filament current controls the temperature of the filament (usually tungsten but occasionally lanthanum hexaboride, LaB_6) and hence the number of electrons emitted.

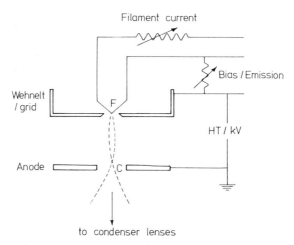

Fig. 4. The thermionic electron gun. Electrons from the filament (F) are accelerated through a hole in the anode. The focusing action of the gun produces a cross-over point, C, from which all electrons appear to come.

In general we want to maximise this number and ensure that all the emitted electrons come from a small region on the filament. In order to achieve this we 'saturate' the filament. This involves increasing the filament current until the number of emitted electrons (the 'beam current') is no longer rising. This can be seen with reference to Fig. 5. We attempt to operate at the 'knee' of the curve (k). We can assess whether this point has been reached either by watching the beam current (on a meter) while turning up the filament current or by studying the shape of a focused electron beam on the screen of the microscope (at a magnification low enough to enable the whole beam to be seen). Fig. 6 shows the characteristic appearance of the beam in a TEM when the filament is under-saturated (at u in Fig. 5), nearly saturated (n in Fig. 5), and fully saturated (s in Fig. 5).

The same effects occur in an SEM but are not so easily made visible. The filament current setting is quite important. The penalty for over-saturating the filament is that the evaporation of tungsten is increased and the filament lifetime is shortened. Incorrect filament saturation can mean the difference between 2 or 3 hours of filament life and the 100 hours which should be attainable in a properly-run instrument.

If the electron gun has a LaB_6 filament then it is necessary to be particularly careful both when installing a new filament and each time the filament is heated up. The emission from a LaB_6 filament is very sensitive to the position of the filament in the Wehnelt assembly and it is worth spending some time adjusting the position of a new filament in order to achieve proper saturation when the filament is heated. A new filament must be 'conditioned' before it is first used. This procedure takes a few hours but is a worthwhile investment of time if the life expectancy of the filament can be extended to a year or more. A typical conditioning procedure consists of raising the filament current by small increments at each available kV setting of the microscope in turn, starting with the lowest. A common practice is to wait 1 minute after each 'click' of the filament current control (or an

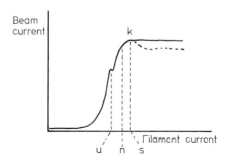

Fig. 5. A graph indicating the way in which the beam current 'emission' increases as the filament current is turned up. The appearance of the fully condensed beam before saturation, near saturation and when fully saturated, is shown in Figs 6 and 38.

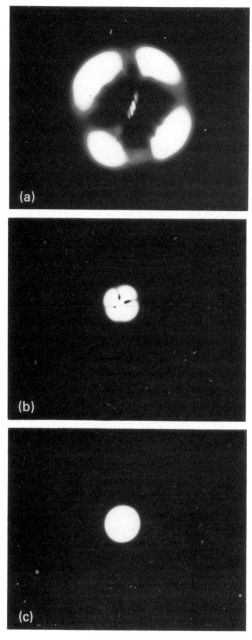

Fig. 6. The appearance on the screen of a fully-focused beam when the filament is (a) under-saturated, (b) nearly saturated and (c) fully-saturated.

equivalent small turn of the knob if it is continuously variable). When the filament is saturated it is left on for five minutes before being turned down again. The procedure is repeated at the next higher kV setting until, a couple of hours later, the gun is operating fully saturated at the highest available kV. It is then important that, each time the filament is switched on, it is heated slowly. If treated carefully, a LaB_6 filament should last for many months.

The second controllable parameter is the gun bias. This controls the total electron current leaving the gun, and the size of the area on the filament from which it comes. Although the source size can be important for high resolution applications the commonest reason for altering the bias setting is to increase or decrease the electron beam current (and hence the apparent brightness of the image). This might be necessary either to decrease the heating and damage caused by the beam (by lowering the bias, i.e. making it more negative) or to improve the visibility of a dark region of the specimen (by increasing the bias). In general a change of bias will affect the saturation of the filament and this may need to be adjusted slightly. However, on some modern instruments the gun bias is linked to the filament current and no further adjustment is necessary. For example on the Philips EM400 series the 'emission' control (equivalent to the gun bias) can be changed without affecting the filament current setting.

The third gun variable is the accelerating voltage (or 'high tension'). This is usually widely variable. For a TEM it can usually be changed in steps from 20 or 40 kV to the maximum of which the instrument is capable (100, 120, 200, 300 or 400 kV). The choice of accelerating voltage will generally be made on the basis of the nature and thickness of the specimen, since higher energy electrons are more penetrating but lead to lower contrast. In an SEM the range available will often stretch from 1 keV to 25 or 30 keV and may be continuously variable. The choice will depend on the depth beneath the surface from which the image is required. However, in addition, more electrons are emitted from the gun at higher voltages. If the accelerating voltage is changed during an operating session it may be necessary to re-establish the other gun parameters and to re-align the microscope column to some extent (see Chapters 3 and 5).

The effects described in this section are summarized in Table 1 and the sequence of steps involved in setting up the gun is re-emphasized in the 'start-up' checklists (front and back cover flaps).

Table 1

Gun variable	Effect of increasing gun variable on:	
	Electron energy	Beam current
kV	up	up
Bias	—	up
Filament current	—	up until knee

It must be emphasized that there is an ultimate limit to the brightness of an electron gun and that higher currents can only in general be drawn at the expense of the spot size or angular divergence of the beam. (For a more detailed discussion see Goodhew and Humphreys, 1988).

1.4. The electromagnetic lens

All of the lenses in a modern microscope operate in the same way. Basically they set up an electromagnetic field symmetrically around the optical axis of the microscope. This is easily done with a simple coil wound round the optical axis (Fig. 7(a)) but in practice the extent of the field needs to be restricted so that the field acts as a 'thin lens' in optical terms. This is achieved by an iron yoke and pole piece (which may be changed quite easily) (Fig. 7(b)). The way in which such a field acts as a converging lens can be seen in Fig. 8. An electron travelling down the optical axis of the microscope A...A experiences no force and continues undeflected. However, an off-axis electron of velocity **v** experiences a force $e(\mathbf{B} \times \mathbf{v})$, i.e. of magnitude $evB\sin\theta$ in the direction perpendicular to both **v** and **B** (into the paper in Fig. 8). This sends the electron spiralling around the optical axis. Once the electron has a component of velocity in a circumferential direction (into the paper), say $\mathbf{v}_c$, then it also experiences a force $e(\mathbf{B} \times \mathbf{v}_c)$ pulling it towards the axis. The electron thus follows a spiral path such as that illustrated in Fig. 8(b). The envelope of this path (shown by the broken line in Fig. 8(b)) is analogous to the familiar ray in the conventional optical diagram (Fig. 8(c)) but in addition the electron rotates through a number of turns of the spiral while traversing the lens. This number is rarely an integer and therefore the electromagnetic lens acts not only to invert the image but

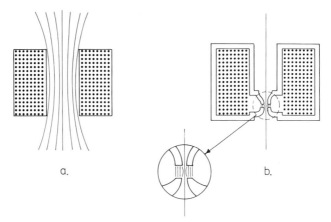

a.   b.

Fig. 7. (a) The field from a simple electromagnet. (b) The field is restricted to the small 'lens' region by the addition of an iron yoke and pole pieces.

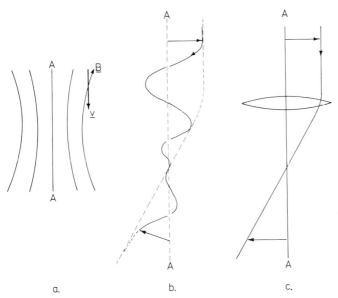

Fig. 8. The action of an electromagnetic lens. (a) The electron with velocity **v** experiences a force $e(\mathbf{B} \times \mathbf{y})$ into the paper. (b) This results in the electron spiralling round the optical axis. Its envelope, shown by the broken line, should be compared with the conventional optical ray diagram (c).

to rotate it about the optical axis by an amount depending on the strength of the lens. Since the great advantage of electron lenses is that their strength (and hence focal length) is easily changed by varying the current through their coil it follows that any variation of the imaging lenses will result in rotation of the image. This effect can be seen in the TEM whenever the magnification (i.e. projector lenses) or focus (i.e. objective lens) is changed and is used to help in aligning the microscope (see Chapter 5).

1.5. Lens aberrations

All simple lenses are subject to aberrations and these are particularly important for electron lenses since the light microscopist's trick of combining lenses of different optical characteristics to make a 'corrected' compound lens is not easily done with electromagnetic lenses. There are two types of aberration which we must consider; chromatic aberration resulting from variations in wavelength (energy) of the electrons and achromatic aberration (principally spherical aberration) arising from the lens geometry or inhomogeneity, even with electrons of a single wavelength (energy). Although in the SEM there are no lenses which act on the image, aberrations are still important. Aberrations in the condenser lenses affect the shape and size of the beam as it hits the specimen and thus affect the resolution and astigmatism of the image.

1.5.1. Chromatic aberration

The dominant effect of chromatic aberration is that the lens brings radiation (i.e. in this case, electrons) of different wavelength (energy) to focus at different points along the optical axis. This is illustrated in Fig. 9, which shows that if a variety of electron energies are present, a lens has no unique focal length and will give rise to a disc of confusion rather than a point focus. This will affect (adversely!) the resolution attainable with the microscope.

The best approach to eliminating chromatic aberration is to use monochromatic electrons (all of the same energy). Good design of electron guns has reduced the spread in energy of the electron beam to a very low value *before it hits the specimen*. However, it is inevitable that some electrons interact with the specimen and lose energy (otherwise we would see no contrast in the TEM). Consequently, there will always be a spread of electron energies through the objective and projector lenses of a TEM and chromatic aberration is unavoidable. This is the most common reason for poor resolution from thick specimens. Although electrons may be transmitted through a thick specimen, if they have lost a significant amount of energy the chromatic aberration effect will reduce the resolution of the image intolerably. Nothing can be done about this except to use a thin specimen or operate at a higher accelerating voltage.

1.5.2. Spherical aberration

Even with perfectly 'monochromatic' electrons a lens will suffer from spherical aberration simply because electrons far from the optical axis must travel further than electrons near the axis. Figure 10 illustrates this. Whereas this aberration can be designed out of light microscopes by combining lenses of different refractive indices, the sole resort in the electron microscope is to use rays which are near the optical axis and thus to minimize the effect. Consequently electron lenses are used at very small apertures compared with light lenses, which accounts for the fact that the microscope column may be about a metre long but only has a 1 mm hole down it for the beam!

1.5.3. Distortion and astigmatism

These two effects arise when the lens system does not perfectly reproduce

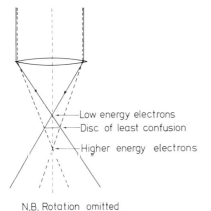

Fig. 9. Chromatic aberration in a lens. The higher energy (shorter-wavelength) electrons are brought to focus further from the lens than those of lower energy. The 'best' focus is not a point but a 'disc of least confusion'.

Fig. 10. Spherical aberration in a lens. Electrons travelling far from the optical axis are brought to focus closer to the lens than electrons near the axis.

the shape of the object. The common distortions are those which make a square appear as a barrel or pincushion (Fig. 11). By and large there is little that the operator can do about this effect—it should have been designed out by the microscope manufacturer. However, it is as well to appreciate that your image may be distorted, especially at low magnification.

Astigmatism arises whenever the lens field is not perfectly symmetrical about the optical axis and results in a 'smearing out' of the image when it is not precisely in focus and an unsharp image when apparently at focus. Figure 12 shows the effect. Astigmatism tends to become worse in an electron microscope as dirt builds up in the column and on the apertures— the non-conducting dirt charges up and distorts the magnetic field of the lens. It is necessary to have correcting coils at various points in the microscope column in order to counteract the asymmetric field and to squeeze

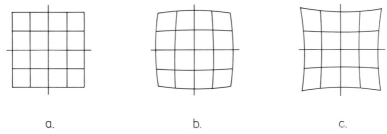

Fig. 11. Common distortions which may be introduced by an optical system, especially at low magnifications. A square (a) may appear as a barrel (b) or a pincushion (c).

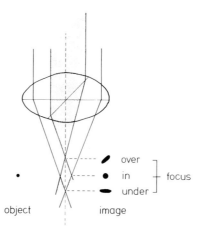

Fig. 12. Astigmatism results when a lens is not perfectly symmetrical. The focus across one diameter is closer to the lens than that across another. This results in a disc of least confusion at 'best' focus. The image of a point object would appear, as shown at the right, as a larger point at best focus but as an image elongated in different directions on each side of focus.

the electron beam back to its symmetrical configuration. This is quite easily carried out using 'quadrupole' or 'octupole' electromagnetic coils, which consist of four or eight small electromagnets arranged around the optical axis. These are activated in such a way that their combined effect is to generate an oval field instead of a circularly symmetrical one. The long axis of the oval can be chosen to counteract the asymmetric astigmatism of the main lens. Figure 13 shows this schematically. The direction of the long axis of the correcting field is controlled via electronic circuits which are set in one of two ways. On most older microscopes the 'orientation' (i.e. θ in Fig. 14) and amplitude, r, (i.e. strength of correcting field) are chosen. On more modern microscopes the alternative convention is commonly used: the strengths of the fields in the x and y directions are chosen (they would need to be approximately equal for the field shown in Fig. 14). Some users find

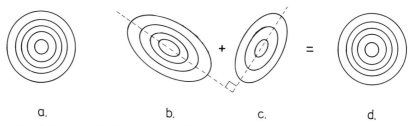

a.   b.   c.   d.

Fig. 13. (a) A schematic diagram of the field of a perfect lens. The optical axis is into the paper. An astigmatic lens will have an elliptical field distribution (b) which can be corrected by adding a small compensating field (c) by means of stigmator coils, to give a resultant symmetric field (d).

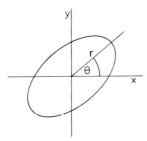

Fig. 14. Illustration of the relationship between orientation and amplitude $(r\theta)$ and (xy) nomenclature for stigmator coils.

the $(x\ y)$ controls easier to use than $(r\ \theta)$ since the two stigmator controls act rather like two subsidiary 'focus' knobs.

1.6. Beam deflectors and scanning coils

We have seen how important it is for all types of microscope that the electron beam travels down the optical axis of the microscope. In order to achieve this in practice it is necessary to be able to deflect the beam at various points in the column. The same requirement, speeded up, exists if the microscope is to be used in any 'scanning' mode, i.e. as a high resolution scanning electron microscope or as a scanning transmission electron microscope (STEM).

Deflection of the beam is simple to arrange using electromagnetic coils whose field lines run across the column. Figure 15 shows the arrangement. Beam deflection is achieved by passing a constant current through the coils whereas scanning of the beam obviously requires a varying current through two sets of coils in the x and y directions. This is usually achieved automatically—the user simply chooses the total time required for one scan (the 'frame' time).

1.7. The complete SEM

We are now in a position to consider the assembly of components into complete microscope systems. The SEM and TEM are considered separately, but with some repetition of material because many readers will, at least initially, wish to read *either* about the SEM *or* the TEM.

Figure 1 shows the majority of the important elements of every SEM. This diagram, and the nomenclature associated with SEMs, are shown on the fold-out flap at the front of this book. The electron gun emits a divergent beam of electrons from its anode hole. Small deflector coils, or alternatively fine mechanical adjustors, enable the beam to be directed down the

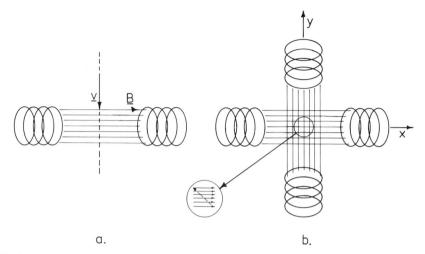

a.   b.

Fig. 15. (a) A single set of deflection coils. An electron travelling downwards (with velocity v shown) will be deflected into the paper. (b) Two sets of coils are used to scan the beam. Here the electron beam is into the paper and the raster usually scanned is shown in the inset.

optical axis of the column. The beam diameter at the specimen is usually controlled by a double condenser lens system, similar to that shown in Fig. 16(a). A first condenser lens (C1), often labelled 'spot size', demagnifies the cross-over of the gun and produces a fine beam. There may be a second condenser lens but it is usually linked to C1 and not controlled independently. The final condenser lens (C2), labelled 'focus' and usually called the objective lens, may then make the beam diameter even smaller, but its main function is to bring the beam to its final cross-over at the plane of the specimen. The diameter of the beam as it hits the specimen is the main factor controlling the resolution of the microscope. Since the setting of C2 is determined by the location of the specimen, primary control of the 'spot size' is exerted by C1. Minor adjustments to the beam diameter can be made by raising or lowering the specimen, which will change the setting of C2 needed to reach focus and therefore its demagnification and spot size. The smaller the 'working distance' (see Fig. 16) the smaller will be the spot size and, potentially, the better the resolution.

A final aperture, which is often the only externally selectable aperture in an SEM column, can be used to control the convergence angle, α_c, of the beam as it hits the specimen. This is shown in Fig. 16(b). The effects of inserting a smaller aperture are threefold:

(i) the total current landing on the specimen is reduced since many electrons are stopped by the aperture,

(ii) the angular convergence is reduced giving a more nearly parallel beam and greater depth of field (Fig. 17), and

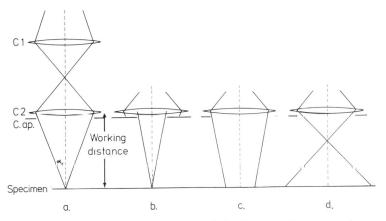

Fig. 16. Double condenser illumination: (a) focused illumination with large condenser aperture; (b) a smaller aperture gives a smaller convergence angle, but fewer electrons; (c) with C2 underfocused the convergence angle is also reduced; (d) with C2 overfocused the electrons all appear to come from the cross-over (see Fig. 21).

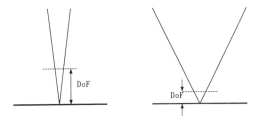

Fig. 17. Illustrating how depth of field (DoF) depends on beam convergence angle. Depth of field is defined as the distance along the optical·axis within which an ideal point in the object is not spread by the microscope into a spot larger than the resolution limit. All points in the object within the DoF thus appear equally sharp in the image.

(iii)   the ultimate beam diameter (spot size) is *increased* because of diffraction at the aperture. The potential resolution of the microscope is thus made worse by selection of a small aperture.

Choice of final aperture size is determined by a compromise between the requirements for strength of signal, depth of field and resolution. In any case the aperture must be centred about the optical axis and the techniques for doing this are described in Chapter 3.

A most important aspect of scanning electron microscopy is that the beam must be scanned or rocked about the specimen. From the earlier discussion of lens aberrations it will be appreciated that the beam should be kept as close to the optical axis of the microscope as possible, particularly in the strong regions of a lens. Scanning is therefore usually achieved using two sets of deflection coils, as indicated in Fig. 18. The position and strength of the coils is arranged so that the beam passes through the final lens and has its pivot point (P), on the optical axis. In most microscopes the scan coils are pre-aligned in the factory and no further alignment by the operator is possible. The final aperture is positioned so that it, too, is as close to the pivot point as possible and thus the size of the aperture controls only the beam convergence and does not interfere with scanning. The correction of astigmatism in an SEM is usually achieved with a single set of adjustment coils, as described in Section 1.5.3, positioned so that they pull the beam into a symmetrical shape which then hits the specimen as a circle.

The secondary signal detector is described in the next section since it critically affects the appearance of the image in the chosen imaging mode. The remaining components of the SEM are electronic. A scan generator controls both the scanning of the beam across the specimen and the synchronous scanning of the spot on the display CRT. The scan generator therefore determines the image magnification, by controlling the size of the region scanned on the specimen while keeping the image in the CRT at a constant size. The signal from the detector is amplified before being used to control the brightness of the CRT spot, and thus the contrast in the image. None of the electronic components need alignment although they may require intelligent setting, as will become evident in Chapter 4.

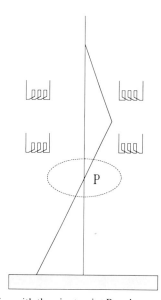

Fig. 18. Normal scanning with the pivot point P at the centre of the objective lens.

1.8. SEM detectors and operating modes

In most modern SEMs the scan generator can be set to make the electron beam produce four distinct types of pattern on the surface of the specimen. These four scan types are:
(i) the rectangular raster, widely used for producing a two-dimensional image,
(ii) the line scan (single or repeated) for studying the variation of a signal along a one-dimensional track on the specimen,
(iii) the stationary spot, used for alignment and to collect data from the smallest possible region of the specimen, and
(iv) the rocked spot, used for collecting crystallographic information (electron channelling patterns).
The fourth, rocking beam, technique requires a little further explanation. The scan coils are energized differently so that the pivot point of the scanned beam is no longer in the centre of the lens (Fig. 18) but at the specimen surface (Fig. 19). This enables the microscopist to sample the signal (often backscattered electrons) as a function of the angle at which the beam strikes the specimen. For crystalline specimens diffraction effects are likely to be seen. The microscopist needs to ensure that the pivot point is actually at the specimen surface and to identify precisely which region on the surface is being illuminated.

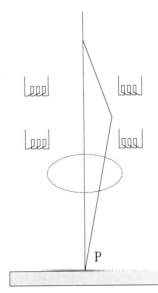

Fig. 19. 'Rocking beam' scanning mode, with the pivot point P at the specimen.

Selection of the signal to be detected is essentially independent of the scanning mode. Most microscopes have two or three different signal detectors (e.g. for secondary electrons, backscattered electrons and X-rays) but several others are possible and will be discussed briefly below. In all cases the primary considerations are that relative positions of the specimen and the detector should permit the beam to hit the specimen and as much as possible of the useful signal to be collected from as large a part of the specimen as possible. Figure 20 illustrates some of the possible problems. If the emitted signal can be attracted towards the detector (e.g. low energy secondary electrons towards a detector biased positive) then there does not have to be a line-of-sight between the region of the specimen hit by the beam and the detector (Fig. 20(a)). On the other hand, if the emitted radiation cannot be deflected easily (e.g. X-rays or light) then line-of-sight and orientation of the specimen become important, since features in shadow will not be 'seen' by the detector. It must be possible to tilt the specimen; this will impose constraints on the position of the detector, and may mean that the detector cannot be installed very close to the specimen. Since detectors are frequently fixed, while specimens can be moved, rotated and tilted with five or six degrees of freedom it is very important that the microscopist knows the whereabouts of the detectors in the microscope chamber.

Secondary electrons are usually detected using an Everhart-Thornley detector positioned typically at S. It consists of a scintillator at a potential in excess of 1 kV behind a metal mesh which can be biased positive (to attract low energy secondaries) or negative (to repel them). Since the secondary electrons can be dragged towards the detector in curved paths (Fig. 20(a)) the position of the detector is not particularly crucial and it does not need

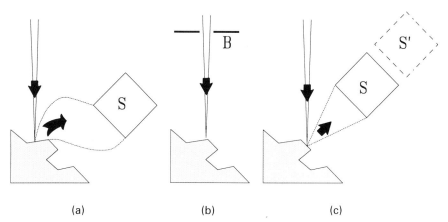

(a)	(b)	(c)

Fig. 20. SEM detectors: (a) Secondary electrons can be attracted by a biased detector (S) and can travel in curved paths. (b) Backscattered electrons only travel in straight lines and the detector (S) needs to be in line of sight. (c) Alternative location for a semiconductor backscattered detector, B.

to be very close to the specimen. It therefore rarely interferes with the specimen.

High energy backscattered electrons can be detected using an Everhart-Thornley detector with its mesh biased negative to repel the low energy secondaries. However, it is more efficient to use a dedicated solid state detector in a position such as B in Fig. 20(b). This position has the advantage that the detector can have a very large collection angle yet is out of the way immediately beneath the pole piece of the final lens. It is very important that the specimen is not accidentally driven upwards into the detector since the scintillator detector is very brittle and is easily damaged.

Cathodoluminescence of the specimen leads to the emission of light, which again travels in straight lines. The intensity of emission from most materials is rather low so the collection efficiency of the detector is of great importance. Common detectors are associated with either fixed paraboloid mirrors or multiple spring-mounted light pipes. If the collector is fixed the position of the specimen is important but if the collectors are flexible they can be positioned to suit the specimen.

X-ray detectors are of course commonplace on modern SEMs. Designers try to arrange them as close to the specimen as possible to maximize their efficiency and a Si(Li) semiconductor detector may be mounted on a sliding mechanism that enables its proximity to the specimen to be controlled. It is evident that a detector at S in Fig. 20(c) will collect a greater fraction of the emitted X-rays than an identical detector at S'. With such a detector it is again particularly important that the microscopist knows the specimen/detector geometry so that the specimen is never driven into the detector.

Other detectors such as specimen-current amplifiers are not mounted in the specimen chamber but rely upon amplifying the current in an earth connection. There is then little operational need to be wary of them.

The best advice to the SEM operator is to familiarize him or herself with the geometry of the specimen and microscope chamber. At the very least, look into the open door of the microscope before loading the specimen. If this is not possible, for instance in an instrument with an airlock, then study diagrams of the specimen chamber carefully and do not exceed the recommended specimen dimension or movement limits.

1.9. The complete TEM

The fold-out flap at the end of the book shows the arrangement of the various components of a TEM side by side with a ray diagram of a straightforward imaging mode. As far as possible the labels have been chosen to correspond to the words printed by the appropriate knobs on JEOL and Philips instruments.

The electron gun, at the top of the column, emits a diverging beam of electrons through the anode hole. This beam is deflected on to the optical axis by the gun deflector coils, controlled by the gun alignment tilt and shift controls. The beam is now focused down to a fairly small spot by the first condenser lens, the setting of which controls the ultimate spot size attainable by the condenser system (generally < 1 μm for a TEM instrument). The function of the second condenser lens is to project the beam at the specimen in such a way that the area illuminated and the convergence angle can be controlled (Fig. 16). The condenser aperture, which is situated below the second condenser lens, effectively controls the number of electrons which are allowed into the beam and hence helps to determine the intensity of the illumination. As a rule the largest aperture ($\geqslant 100$ μm) is only needed for thick specimens and for X-ray analysis, whereas a medium aperture (≈ 50 μm) provides adequate illumination for most specimens. The smallest apertures (30 μm or less) reduce the illumination level considerably but are needed to give the best resolution and the least beam damage. Resolution and image sharpness are improved if condenser 2 is operated in the overfocused condition shown in Fig. 16(d) (i.e. if the illumination is spread by turning the condenser 2 knob clockwise and exciting the lens more strongly). The reason for this is illustrated in Fig. 21. When the condenser is focused (Fig. 21(a)) the area of interest R is being illuminated by a cone of electrons of semi-angle α_c controlled by the aperture size and all information in the image is 'smeared out' through this angle. However, when the condenser is overfocused (Fig. 21(b)) the same area, R, receives electrons only from the cross-over point, where the beam diameter is much smaller than the condenser aperture and hence α_c is much reduced.

Below the condenser aperture is the condenser stigmator, whose function is to compensate for astigmatism in the illumination system and to create a circular beam profile at the specimen. At approximately the same place in the column 'wobbler' coils act as a focusing aid (see Chapter 6) and two

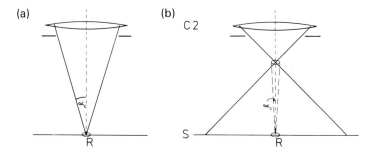

Fig. 21. The effect of overfocusing the second condenser lens C2. The region of the specimen in which we are interested is within the circle R. With C2 in focus (a) this is illuminated by a beam of convergence angle α_c. If C2 is overfocused (b) the electrons all come from the small crossover region and α_c is much reduced.

sets of alignment coils are positioned to bring the beam exactly on to the optical axis in the crucial part of the microscope near the specimen. If the microscope is equipped for scanning, the scan coils will also be in this part of the column.

The specimen, objective aperture, and objective stigmator coils all sit inside the objective lens windings and space is very tight in this part of the column. The objective lens focuses on the specimen and forms an intermediate image at a magnification of about 50 ×. The objective aperture sits in the 'back focal plane' of the lens and enables the operator to allow particular groups of electrons to contribute to the final image (Chapter 6). Figure 22 shows two ray diagrams of this region.

In the plane of the first intermediate image is the 'selected area' or 'diffraction' aperture which allows a particular part of the image to be selected for examination or, more usually, for electron diffraction. It is not practicable to select a region of interest at the specimen plane for two reasons: the column is already cluttered with hardware in the neighbourhood of the specimen and also, selection of a region in the intermediate image is physically much easier because this image is fifty times larger than the specimen. Consequently, a region 1 μm in diameter can be selected using an aperture which is actually 50 μm across. In practice apertures such as have been described are simply circular holes in thin sheets of platinum, molybdenum or gold.

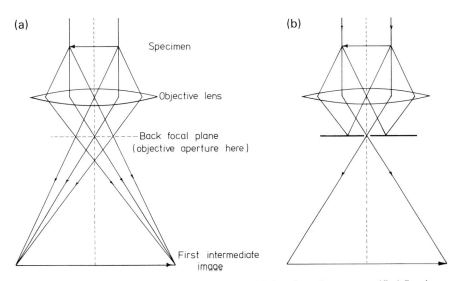

Fig. 22. The objective lens. The main function of this lens is to form a magnified first intermediate image. In the back focal plane of the lens a diffraction pattern is formed. (a) All rays leaving the specimen parallel go through a single point in the diffraction pattern. (b) Insertion of an objective aperture in the back focal plane eliminates diffracted electrons from the image.

Below the diffraction aperture are three or four lenses whose function is to magnify the central part of the image or the diffraction pattern and project it on to the fluorescent screen. These lenses are used in a variety of combinations but not necessarily all at one time. Finally a shutter and camera are located below the fluorescent screen. Although special film is often used in electron microscopes it is always sensitive to light as well as electrons and therefore photography must be performed in a darkened room.

1.10. Common TEM operating modes

Most electron miscroscopes offer many alternative imaging possibilities. Perhaps the most used is high magnification imaging, shown in the ray diagram on the back cover flap. However, there are many other configurations, of which the commonest are usually selectable by a single push button and will be described here.

1.10.1. Low magnification

When low magnifications are required, one or more lenses may be switched off or alternatively several of the lenses may be excited more weakly. This latter approach has the advantage that the various distortions which tend to occur when a lens is used at low magnification (see Section 1.5.3) can be made to cancel out, giving a final distortion-free image.

On most microscopes a single magnification knob provides magnifications from $100\times$ to the top instrument magnification which may be $300\,000\times$ or more. In this case, different lenses will be brought into action for different magnification ranges. Whenever a lens is switched on or off the image visible on the screen rotates through $180°$ since one extra or one fewer image inversions is now operating. Figure 23 illustrates the image inversions which occur on the JEOL 200 CX as the magnification is gradually turned up from $6000\times$ to $450\,000\times$. At first (Fig. 23(a)) the objective lens is excited weakly and presents a virtual image to the weak 'intermediate 1' lens. The second intermediate lens is off and the projector lens presents an upright final image (upright that is except for the inevitable rotations in each lens which are hard to draw in a diagram!). At higher magnifications (Fig. 23(b)) the objective lens is strengthened and the second intermediate lens is switched on. The final image is now inverted. At still higher magnifications both intermediate lenses are excited strongly and another image inversion occurs, giving a final upright image again (Fig. 23(c)). This rotates slowly as the magnification is increased and the strength of the intermediate lenses rises.

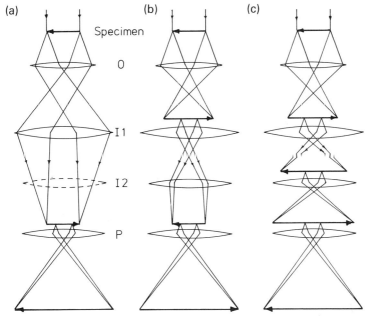

Fig. 23. Three of the commonly used optical configurations of the JEOL JEM200CX microscope, illustrating the many image inversions which may occur. (a) At low magnification the second intermediate lens (I2) is switched off. (b) At intermediate magnifications all lenses are on and there are three image inversions. (c) At high magnification all lenses are strongly excited and there are four image inversions.

1.10.2. Diffraction modes

All transmission microscopes offer the ability to view the diffraction pattern which inevitably forms in the back focal plane of the objective lens (Fig. 22(a)). Even if the user is not particularly interested in electron diffraction from the specimen, this is a useful facility for aligning the objective aperture (see Chapter 5). In the back focal plane of the objective lens all parallel 'rays' leaving the specimen in a specific direction pass through a point in the 'diffraction pattern'. Three examples of such sets of rays are shown in Fig. 22. In normal operation the diffraction pattern is unseen because the first intermediate lens is focused on the first intermediate image (bottom of Fig. 22(a)) and this is what is finally projected on to the screen. It is simple to change the excitation of the intermediate lenses so that they present magnified versions of the diffraction pattern to the projector system. This is so frequently required that a single button is normally provided to enable the user to view the diffraction pattern at any time. The ray diagram is now of the type shown in Fig. 24(b). Notice that the excitation of the objective lens does not change between the image setting (Fig. 24(a))

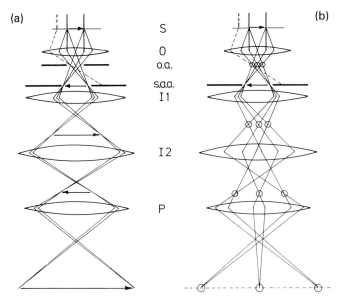

(a)

(b)

S

O

o.a.

s.a.a.

I1

I2

P

Fig. 24. A comparison of optical configurations in (a) high magnification imaging and (b) selected area diffraction. It should be noted that (a) is essentially the same as Fig. 23(c). The ray indicated by broken lines in both (a) and (b) is stopped by the selected area aperture (s.a.a.), illustrating that the diffraction pattern in (b) can arise only from the selected area.

and the diffraction setting (Fig. 24(b)). The objective aperture must be removed in order for all of the diffraction pattern to be visible and Fig. 24 shows that the 'selected area' aperture in the plane of the first intermediate image can be used to select the region of the object from which the diffraction pattern is formed. It is important for accurate diffraction work that the intermediate lenses are at their correct settings and the methods of achieving this are discussed in Chapter 5.

1.10.3. Scanning modes

Many modern TEMs can be used in a scanning mode, either in transmission (STEM) or using secondary emission (SEM). In each case the instrumental resolution is limited by the electron beam diameter at the specimen and a much finer beam is needed than for conventional TEM. The way in which such scanning microscopes form an image has been dealt with earlier in this chapter. However it is necessary to consider here the way in which the basic TEM components are used to provide a fine scanned beam. The general approach is to use the condenser system to create a fairly fine beam (by using a strongly excited first condenser lens) and then to increase the excitation of the specially designed objective lens until it acts both as an objective and as a final condenser. Then, with the addition of scanning coils between the condenser and objective lenses, the system operates as shown diagrammatically in Fig. 25.

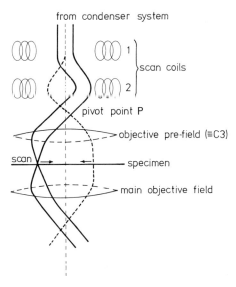

Fig. 25. An idealized diagram of the operation of a TEM/STEM in STEM mode. The beam is scanned between the full and broken lines.

In this diagram the strong objective lens is shown as two lenses—the pre-field acts as a third condenser lens while the main lens action is that of a normal objective lens. The two sets of scanning coils are needed to cause the beam to appear to pivot about the point P but the objective lens pre-field causes the beam to hit the specimen at virtually the same angle throughout its scan. The lenses further down the microscope are not generally crucial to the imaging—their main function in the STEM mode is to direct all the transmitted electrons to a detector to be counted, which is quite easily done. The combination of strong objective lens excitation, particular condenser settings and the activation of the scan coils is all normally achieved automatically when the microscope is switched to STEM or SEM operation. However, it is important that the beam is initially aligned on the optical axis of the microscope and that the pivot point is appropriate. These alignments are discussed in Chapter 7.

2 The vacuum system

The vacuum system of an electron microscope exists for two reasons. First, it is essential to remove most of the air from the column of the microscope in order to minimize the scattering of the electron beam by gas molecules and permit the electrons to travel from gun to specimen and camera, a distance of about a metre. This requirement is easily met by a relatively modest vacuum system providing pressures of 10^{-4} Torr (10^{-2} Pa) or better throughout the column. The second reason for the vacuum system is more rigorous, however. It is to prevent the specimen, the apertures, or the electron gun becoming contaminated by the deposition of any atomic or molecular material which may be in the column. It is impractical to 'prevent' contamination but modern vacuum systems and 'anti-contamination' devices are designed to minimize the effect by removing as many molecular species as possible from the residual gas in the microscope column. This is normally achieved using a combination of four types of pumping device. We shall briefly describe each of these and then go on to suggest how the microscope user can help them to be effective.

2.1. The rotary pump

The simplest mechanical pump sweeps gas out using rotating vanes immersed in an oil tank. This is relatively cheap but quite noisy and is usually used to 'rough-pump' the microscope before other pumps are used and to 'back-up' or 'back' diffusion pumps (see below). The main snags to the rotary pump are noise, smell, vibration and a tendency to wear out drive belts and bearings. For these reasons rotary pumps are situated as far from the microscope as is feasible and may be operated only intermittently when absolutely necessary.

2.2. Turbomolecular pumps

Many microscopes are now available with just a single turbomolecular pump, often backed by a small rotary pump. The turbomolecular pump operates as a very rapidly-rotating fan which sweeps gas molecules out of the pumping line. Its great advantages are that all pumping, from almost atmospheric pressure to better than 10^{-5} Torr, can be achieved using a single pump which should in principle introduce no contaminating oils into the system. Its disadvantages are associated with the extremely high rotational speeds which are needed. The fan whines audibly as it starts up, pumps gas and, more seriously, the fan bearings need regular maintenance and tend not to have a long life.

2.3. Diffusion pumps

Diffusion pumps contain oil or mercury which is heated until it gives off a significant amount of vapour. This is then directed by fixed vanes in such a way that it encourages gas molecules from the vacuum system to diffuse towards an exit which is pumped ('backed') by a rotary pump or by a large vacuum reservoir. Diffusion pumps will not begin to operate unless the pressure is below 10^{-1} Torr (10 Pa) and consequently the microscope must first be roughly evacuated using a rotary pump. The disadvantage of a diffusion pump is that it is difficult to eliminate its vapour entirely from the microscope column and it is also disastrous if air comes into contact with hot oil—the correct pumping sequence must be maintained. In some SEMs (and the latest TEMs) the combination of rotary and diffusion pumps is being replaced by a turbomolecular pump.

2.4. Ion pumps

These pumps rely on the fact that ionized gases can be attracted towards an electrode. If that electrode is receptive to gas atoms and molecules (i.e. acts as a getter), then we have an ion getter pump. This type of pump is cleaner than a diffusion pump but again cannot operate well at atmospheric pressure and so needs to be 'backed'.

2.5. Cryopumps

Cryogenic pumps operate because gas atoms will condense on a sufficiently cold surface and thus are removed from the vapour phase. Cryopumping is not widely used in TEMs to pump the conventional gases but is extensively used in the form of 'anti-contamination devices' to remove larger molecules from the column. Thus copper plates cooled by liquid nitrogen are often installed near the specimen and above the oil diffusion pump. Clearly they only work while cooled and if allowed to warm up to room temperature will boil off most of the gas previously condensed onto them.

2.6. The complete microscope system

As an example of the way in which these pumps may be combined in a TEM, Fig. 26 shows the pumping scheme for the Philips EM400T. The

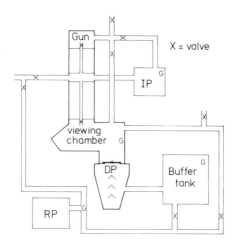

Fig. 26. A simplified diagram of the vacuum system of the Philips EM400T. The camera is pumped by an oil diffusion pump (DP) while the gun and specimen areas are pumped by an ion getter pump (IP). All areas are roughed initially by a rotary pump (RP). This also maintains the vacuum in the buffer tank which backs the diffusion pump. Vacuum gauges monitor the pressure at points labelled G.

microscope is divided into four sections, each of which can be isolated. The crucial column components need rarely be exposed to air, since the gun filament, the photographic film, and the specimen can all be changed via airlocks.

A rotary pump is used to rough-pump each of the four sections and to keep the reservoir pressure below 10^{-1} Torr (10 Pa). When it is not needed for any of these purposes, it automatically cuts out. An oil diffusion pump, backed by the reservoir, pumps the main part of the camera chamber and column. The sensitive areas of the gun and specimen chambers are additionally pumped by the ion getter pump. In practice the user need scarcely be aware of these pumping arrangements since the pumping sequence is automatic and safety devices ensure that the microscope cannot be operated until an appropriate vacuum is reached.

2.7. Contamination

Despite all the pumping arrangements some hydrocarbon and silicone molecules always remain in the microscope column. The most serious manifestation of their presence is the build up of 'contamination' on the specimen as the molecules are cracked by the electron beam and solids are deposited. Liquid nitrogen cooled anti-contaminators in the pumping lines or around the specimen can do much to reduce this effect. However, it must be realized that much of the 'contamination' enters the column not via the pump but attached to the specimen or the operator's hands. Reduction of contamination is a matter not only of good microscope pumping maintenance but also of clean specimen preparation and careful handling of components which will enter the microscope vacuum. It is therefore desirable to handle with gloves or lint-free tissue such components as the specimen stage, the Wehnelt assembly and the camera plate holders. It is also useful to admit dry nitrogen rather than the inevitably damp laboratory air when any part of the system needs to be vented.

3 SEM alignment procedures

Scanning electron microscopes vary greatly in their complexity. They may differ in the number of condenser lenses, range of accelerating voltages, scan speeds and signal manipulation facilities, although their ultimate resolving power varies over only a small range. Because of this great variety, the details of the total alignment procedures will not be the same for all instruments. However, there are several general principles which are described here, together with particular reference to some of the commonly available microscopes.

The brightness of the final image viewed on the display screen is a function of many variables. This can be seen by considering Fig. 1 (or front cover flap). The number of electrons in the final beam is a function of the accelerating voltage, condenser lens settings and final aperture (all electron optical controls). The number of electrons which are emitted from the surface of the specimen will depend on the specimen composition, density, and surface topography and the proportion of these electrons which reach the detector will depend on the specimen/detector geometry. From this point the brightness and contrast of the signal (and thus of the image) will be controlled electronically by the gain of the detector (e.g. photomultiplier tube) and then by subsequent amplification of the signal. Finally, the brightness and contrast of the display CRT can be adjusted for personal preference depending on background room illumination. If one considers a single line scan across the specimen the output signal displayed on a CRT should look similar to that shown in Fig. 27. The mean level of the signal represents the BRIGHTNESS and the height from peak to trough the CONTRAST. Changing the CONTRAST of the signal will usually only change the height of the peaks but changing the BRIGHTNESS may sometimes give the appearance of changing both brightness and contrast.

If the contrast of the image is too high and detail is being lost in the 'white' or 'black' regions a GAMMA control is usually available which will 'compress' the total signal. A value of GAMMA = 1 means that the output signal is unchanged and GAMMA = 3 means that the output signal is the cube root of the input signal. A high value of GAMMA therefore produces a low contrast signal.

Many instruments have an automatic brightness control which will maintain the brightness of the signal to compensate for changes to the electron optics such as accelerating voltage or spot size. It is wise to turn this off when first learning to operate the microscope, as it may mask the effect of some of the changes you make. However, if the autobrightness control

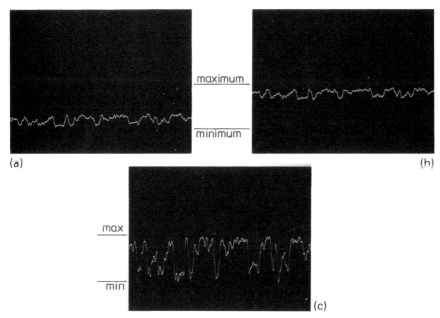

Fig. 27. The effect of brightness and contrast on a single line trace across the specimen: (a) represents a low level of brightness, (b) shows the increase in signal level as brightness is increased and (c) shows the further effect of increasing contrast.

provides the only means of changing the brightness (e.g. on the Cambridge S100) then it is advisable to remain in this mode for the majority of the alignment procedures only switching to manual brightness for filament alignment.

Specimen position is very important when first aligning the microscope, since most SEM specimen chambers are spacious and allow the loading of multiple specimens or of one very large sample. Careful attention must be paid to the relative positions of specimen, detector, and final lens. This is illustrated in Fig. 28 for both tilted and flat specimens. As can be seen in Fig. 28(a) a region at the top of the specimen is the area to be examined. The WORKING DISTANCE (usually displayed on the microscope console) is the distance from the final lens to the specimen region in focus i.e. that being viewed. If the specimen is in an inappropriate position there is a high probability that the specimen will damage either the final lens or a backscattered electron detector. Similarly, Fig. 28(b) shows that when viewing the specimen flat there is a danger that in attempting to view a region at the left of the sample the specimen will be driven into the secondary electron detector. For these reasons it is important to understand the geometry of the specimen chamber and specimen.

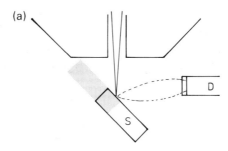

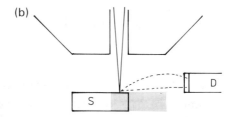

Fig. 28. Potential hazards of specimen movement. (a) A tilted specimen (S) can unwittingly be driven upwards (shaded position) until it hits the objective lens. (b) A flat specimen (S) can be moved until it may strike the detector (D).

3.1. The illumination system

In an SEM the term *'illumination system'* covers the entire electron optical system since all the lenses are used to form a probe at the specimen. However, it is normal practice to consider the first lenses as the CONDENSER lenses and the final lens as the OBJECTIVE lens as this is used only to focus the image rather than to change the spot size. Many SEMs have more than one lens to alter the spot size but these are often coupled to one control called SPOT SIZE or RESOLUTION. These lenses are only decoupled for diffraction operation (e.g. for the rocking beam mode, Section 1.8). Wherever possible in the following descriptions of alignment procedures, each control will be referred to by its function. A list of common names given to these controls by the microscope manufacturers is to be found in the nomenclature chart inside the front cover.

3.2. The electron gun

The way in which a thermionic gun works has been described in Section 1.3. It should not be assumed that the last user left the instrument in a conventional manner and thus before starting to turn on the gun it may be helpful to set the following initial conditions:

MAGNIFICATION	Low (e.g. 100 ×)
SPOT SIZE	Medium (e.g. midpoint)
SCAN SPEED	Fast (TV rate if available)
CONTRAST	Minimum
GAMMA	1
kV	20 approx.
SPECIMEN	Known test
AUTOBRIGHTNESS	Off/manual

Now switch on the filament at the lowest setting and slowly increase its value at the same time viewing the CRT or the FILAMENT EMISSION METER (if fitted). Once an image is observed then align the filament by one of the following three methods.

METHOD 1

This assumes that it is possible to select a LINE SCAN so that the beam is scanning along a single line. The SIGNAL from this will be displayed either on the normal viewing CRT or on a WAVEFORM MONITOR. The changes in SIGNAL with increase of FILAMENT CURRENT can be seen in Fig. 29. At low values of FILAMENT CURRENT the trace should show some contrast (Fig. 29(a)). As the FILAMENT CURRENT is increased, so both brightness and contrast will increase (Fig. 29(b)). If the gun is well aligned the SIGNAL will reach a maximum value at saturation and any further increase in FILAMENT CURRENT will only reduce the filament life but not increase the brightness. If the gun is not aligned then the SIGNAL will reach a peak value and then decrease with increase of FILA-MENT CURRENT (Fig. 29(c)). When this happens take the FILAMENT CURRENT to just past peak value and using the GUN TILT controls maxi-mize the SIGNAL. Slowly increase the FILAMENT CURRENT and repeat using the GUN TILT until saturation is achieved. Return to normal scan mode.

METHOD 2

Some microscopes do not have a LINE SCAN mode and thus the satura-tion of the beam can only be achieved by viewing the CRT. As in method 1, slowly increase the FILAMENT CURRENT to obtain maximum bright-ness on the CRT. If the brightness decreases beyond a certain filament current, align the gun using the GUN TILT CONTROLS. (These controls may be either electrical or manual). Again, once maximum brightness has been achieved on the CRT, check that further increases in FILAMENT CURRENT do not result in a loss of brightness. If this happens repeat the alignment until saturation is obtained.

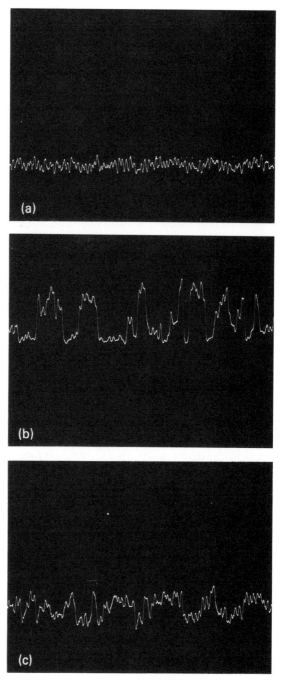

Fig. 29. The line traces which should be seen when the filament is (a) undersaturated, (b) saturated, and (c) at higher filament current when the gun is misaligned.

METHOD 3

This is an unusual method found, for example, on some of the Cambridge instruments. It relies on the imaging of the filament and the various stages can be seen in Fig. 30. Saturation position is now determined by the size of the 'filament image'. Once the correct value of FILAMENT CURRENT has been obtained (i.e. the smallest spot) the 'image' is centred using the GUN TILT controls. This method has the advantage that since an image is visible on the CRT the SPOT SIZE can be set to maximum while the GUN TILTS are centred. The SPOT SIZE can then be reduced and any movement of the 'image' corrected using the GUN SHIFT controls. Finally, switch back to AUTOBRIGHTNESS if this facility is available.

3.3. Final aperture alignment

No mention has yet been made of focusing the image since this was not necessary to achieve the previous alignment. The image should now be focused using the FOCUS control, at a magnification of about $500 \times$ (e.g. Fig. 31(a)). Decide on the working distance (between specimen and final lens) to be used. This will typically be 15 mm, giving medium resolution and depth of field. 'Rock' the image by changing FOCUS through the in-focus position. If the image moves across the CRT or appears to rotate about a point *not* at the centre (Fig. 31(e)), this means that the final aperture is misaligned (Fig. 31(d)); the image should merely rotate about the screen centre. Whilsts 'rocking' the image through focus adjust the X and Y aperture controls until only rotation (rather than translation) of the image occurs. Figure 31(c) gives an impression of what this should look like on the screen: the aperture will now be centred around the optical axis (Fig. 31(b)). If the SEM is fitted with a 'WOBBLE' control this will automatically rock the image through focus.

Once the APERTURE has been aligned at low magnification, repeat the alignment procedure at the SPOT SIZE required and at a higher magnification. Since many microscopes permit only limited alignment of the condenser lenses, final aperture alignment tends to be a frequent event.

Some of the Cambridge SEMs have an Optibeam mode which automatically adjusts the settings of the condenser lenses to optimize their value for a given aperture and spot size setting. It is possible to use this mode to change the effective angular aperture without changing the physical aperture or working distance. It may still be necessary to align the aperture when using this Optibeam mode of operation.

3.4. Image astigmatism

This alignment is absolutely critical if the highest resolution is needed.

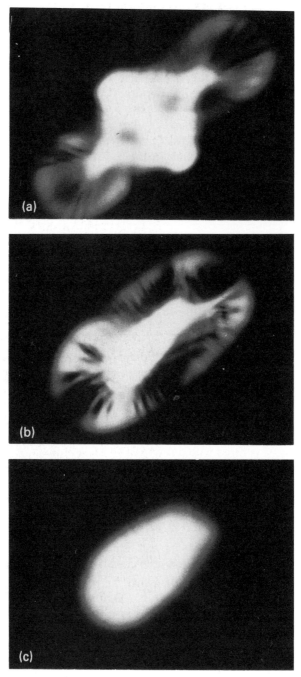

Fig. 30. The appearance of the beam on the screen of a Cambridge SEM in alignment mode when the filament is (a) undersaturated, (b) almost saturated, at the 'knee' and (c) fully saturated.

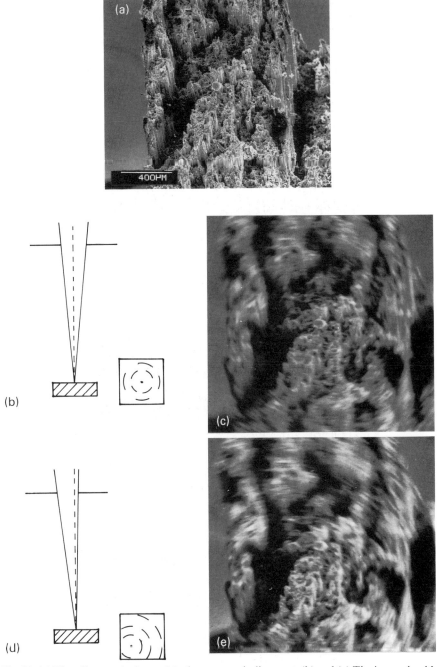

Fig. 31. (a) The effect on the image (a) of aperture misalignment. (b) and (c) The image should rotate about the centre of the screen when the focus is altered. If the aperture is not centred on the optical axis the image no longer rotates (on focusing) about the centre of the screen (d) and (e).

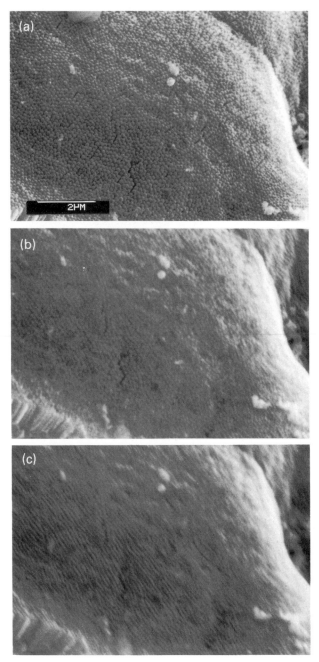

Fig. 32. The reduction of image quality with astigmatism. (a) The astigmatism is corrected, clearly resolving the microvilli on conventionally fixed pig gut. (b) There is slight astigmatism resulting in a loss of sharpness. (c) Gross astigmatism results in distortion of image features.

Astigmatism has been described in Section 1.5.3. and its effect on an image can vary from making circular objects appear elliptical to a general loss of sharpness of the image. Figure 32(a) shows an in-focus corrected image of microvilli on a pig gut. Figure 32(b) is also in focus but the presence of slight astigmatism has resulted in a loss of sharpness. In Fig. 32(c) the image is very astigmatic and distortion of the small features is seen. Correction of astigmatism is best made by considering the two 'stigmator' controls as fine focus controls. The following procedure is usually adopted.

   (i) Select a suitable magnification (say 20 000 × since astigmatism should not be visible at low magnification).

 (ii) Adjust SPOT SIZE to give a small spot compatible with high resolution.

(iii) FOCUS the image.

(iv) 'Refocus' using the ASTIGMATISM CONTROLS.

 (v) Focus the image using the FOCUS controls.

Repeat steps (iii), (iv), and (v) until the sharpest image is obtained. On going through focus no 'linearity' of features at right angles should now be observed. If a higher magnification is required repeat the procedure at a magnification setting higher than that at which you intend to photograph the image.

3.5. Condenser lens alignment

Many instruments do not require the user to align the condenser lenses, but for those which do require alignment for optimum resolution the following procedure as used on the JEOL 35CF may act as a guide.

   (i) Align the gun and final aperture, as described in the previous section, at 25 kV.

 (ii) Reduce the CONDENSER LENS to minimum. *Take care not to flood the photomultiplier. Switch to backscattered mode.*

(iii) Centre illumination by centring the CONDENSER LENS.

(vi) Reduce accelerating voltage to 5 kV.

 (v) Centre illumination with BEAM SHIFT controls.

Repeat steps (iii), (iv), and (v) until no movement of illumination occurs with change of accelerating voltage. The SEM should now be ready for use.

4 SEM operating procedures

It is useful to have a standard set of conditions under which one can compare the day to day performance of the instrument but these conditions should not be regarded as the normal operating conditions since far more information can be obtained from a specimen if several of the operating parameters are intelligently varied.

4.1. Accelerating voltage

The lower the accelerating voltage the lower the energy of the electrons impinging on the surface of the specimen. If the specimen has a tendency to charge then the use of a lower kV is likely to reduce the problem and if the kV is selected carefully the point of charge balance may be reached at which the number of electrons hitting the surface equals the number of electrons emitted. At this value there will be no charging of the specimen and therefore most specimens can be examined without gold or carbon coating. However, there will be a loss of signal because the uncoated specimen in general produces fewer secondary electrons and the lower beam current results in a loss of primary electrons. Also, there will almost certainly be a reduction in resolution for most SEMs operating with a thermionic gun where the best resolution is obtained at 20 to 30 keV.

A second, but less frequently exploited, criterion is the need to look at the specimen surface. It is often assumed by novice operators that since secondary electrons have a very low energy (significantly less than 50eV) only surface detail is revealed. This is not always the case and is very clearly illustrated in the example used by Chapman (1986). A TEM specimen consisting of a very thin carbon film supported on a copper grid is viewed in the SEM at various kVs.

Figure 33 shows that at the higher accelerating voltages the grid is clearly visible although the support film is not, but at the lowest kV only the support film, not the grid, is observed. This is of course only a test specimen but it indicates what one might see at low and high kV if a sample was covered with a thin surface film.

It is, therefore, recommended that all specimens are initially viewed at a low accelerating voltage to observe the real surface structure and the accelerating voltage is only increased (with surface coating of the specimen as required) when one is satisfied that there is no loss in specimen information at the higher accelerating voltage.

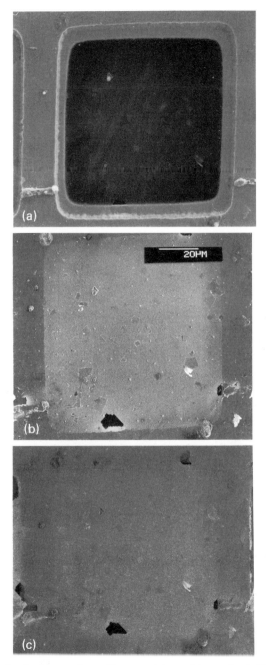

Fig. 33. Changes in the image of a grid covered by a thin mesh at different accelerating voltages. (a) At 20 kV the grid bars are the main feature, whereas (b) at 2.5 kV both mesh and underlying grid bars are visible. (c) At 1 kV only the mesh is visible but the reduced resolution means that some detail is lost.

To optimize the signal at the lower kVs it may be neessary to reduce the anode to cathode distance and this will almost certainly be achieved by replacing the anode with one of different geometry. Since this will normally require venting the microscope to air to replace or adjust the anode, followed by repumping and subsequent realignment, a delay in operation of about ten minutes will be involved but the improvement in signal will compensate for the loss of time. At low accelerating voltages any problems from contamination in the column will also be highlighted, rendering astigmatism correction difficult.

4.2. Spot size

The smaller the diameter of the electron beam the better the potential instrumental resolution, but a reduction in probe size is accompanied by a reduction in beam current which means fewer secondary electrons are emitted and thus the image will be 'noisy'. It is therefore very important to optimize the spot size for the magnification used. Instrument manufacturers tend not to calibrate the spot size control in actual values of the beam diameter since this is not only dependent on condenser lens settings but also on accelerating voltage, final aperture, and working distance. It thus becomes a matter of experience and trial and error to find the required value. In seeking the highest resolution, it may help to select a magnification at least four times the required value; then to reduce spot size gradually (increase the strength of the condenser lens) until there is no change in the 'noise' level. This will be close to the optimum size. Remember that viewing at TV scan rates will always produce a 'noisy' image for small spot sizes, and corrections to image alignments (e.g. astigmatism) will be easier at slower scan rates and with a reduced raster size. If a lower magnification picture is also required, increase the spot size since otherwise the resolution of the image at these lower magnifications will also be reduced. This is illustrated in Fig. 34 where three different spot sizes and three different magnifications have been selected. At the highest magnification (30 000 ×) and smallest spot size the image is crisp and edge detail is clearly visible. As the spot size is reduced the highest magnification image shows a loss of image quality but the remaining two magnifications are unimpaired. A further reduction in spot size then reduces the quality of the intermediate magnification image. In all cases the quality of the lowest magnification image is unaffected by the changes in spot size but the reduction of 'noise' is a positive advantage.

The spot size may be dictated by the specimen since delicate samples may not tolerate the increased electron flux in a large spot and hence it may be necessary to use smaller spot sizes than the magnification would suggest.

4.3. Aperture

The angular aperture is affected by both the physical size of the aperture and the working distance (see Fig. 35). Selection of the aperture is made depending on the conflicting needs for resolution or depth of field. In general, a smaller aperture is required to increase depth of field and this will reduce the number of electrons at the specimen. However, if a large depth of focus is required this will normally mean that one is working at lower magnifications and therefore an increase in spot size to counter-balance this loss of signal can be tolerated. If the instrument is fitted with a multi-aperture holder a range of aperture sizes is available and selection for optimum imaging is achieved very easily. However, if there is only one aperture this is normally selected for resolution and a reduction in angular aperture can only be achieved by increasing the working distance.

4.4. Focusing

In direct contrast to TEM imaging, there is nothing to be gained by de-focusing an SEM image. Since in an SEM the focus setting is unaffected by changes in magnification, it is usually convenient to focus at a magnification several times that used for photography.

It is common practice to view the specimen while it is tilted at 45° towards the detector and normally with the very large depth of field of an SEM the entire image will be in focus. However, if a very high tilt angle has been selected (for example to improve the visibility of very small steps on a polished surface) then a change in focus will be observed from top to bottom of the screen. To reduce this many microscopes are fitted with what is usually called 'Dynamic focus'. This means that the focus setting can be automatically changed as the beam scans from top to bottom of the image. A typical procedure is to focus the image at screen centre and then view a line profile from the top of the screen and 'focus' this with the dynamic focus control; then as the photograph is taken the objective lens changes between these limits keeping the entire field in focus.

4.5. Magnification

As with all microscopes, the magnification selected for the micrograph should be the minimum required to observe the necessary detail. Further photographic magnification is possible for display purposes but cannot improve the resolution. Many SEMs have a dual magnification mode which allow a selected part of the screen to be viewed and photographed at a

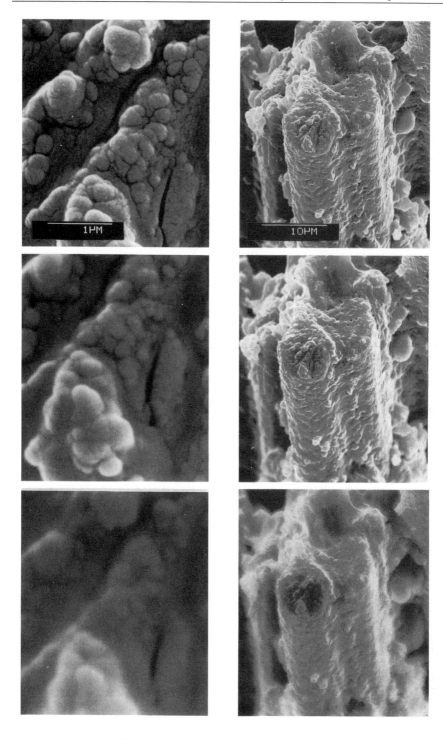

small
spot size

medium
spot size

large
spot size

Fig. 34. The relationship between spot size (increasing *down* each column), magnification (highest on the left), and resolution.

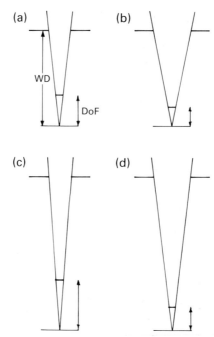

Fig. 35. The effect of aperture size and working distance (WD) on the depth of field. Increasing WD (a–c and b–d) increases depth of field, shown by the vertical arrow. Increasing the aperture diameter (a–b and c–d) reduces the depth of field.

higher magnification. This is a very useful feature enabling fine detail to be observed in context to its surroundings.

The magnification across a field of view will also depend on specimen tilt. For example at $10\,000 \times$ the magnification in the X direction will be $10\,000 \times$ but in the Y direction it will be $(10/1.414)\,000 \times$ for a specimen tilt of $45°$ (Fig. 36). There are two ways to eliminate this distortion:

(i) photograph the specimen flat (untilted), or
(ii) use a tilt correction accessory to stretch the image according to the tilt angle selected (beware of the calibration of tilt, see Fig. 37).

Although, as emphasized in the previous section, it is normal to focus the image at a higher magnification than will be needed for photography this can lead to problems. If the sample is beam sensitive the reduced area scanned at the higher magnification may become damaged due to the increased electron dose. If this does occur focusing on a region slightly to one side of the region to be photographed may help. Check that you only move away from the chosen region in a direction which will not alter the focus setting.

Similar problems may occur if the surface has become contaminated with

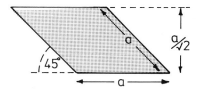

Fig. 36. Foreshortening due to specimen tilt. A square region viewed at 45° is foreshortened by a factor $\sqrt{2}$ in the direction of tilt.

an organic solvent and then a carbon contamination mark may be seen at lower magnifications.

4.6. Specimen tilt

Traditionally when using the SEM the sample is tilted at 45° towards the secondary detector to increase the number of electrons reaching the detector. If one considers the specimen/detector geometry shown in Fig. 28 the increase in signal is due mainly to an increase in the number of back-scattered electrons (not secondary electrons) and thus tilting the specimen improves topographical detail but almost certainly reduces the image resolution.

4.7. Secondary/backscattered electrons

All SEMs are fitted with a secondary electron detector and usually this can be biased negative to provide a limited ability to detect backscattered electrons. This image mode may enhance topographical detail. With a dedicated backscattered detector as described in Section 1.8, there is the added advantage that the signal from separate quadrants can be *added* to give compositional information. In this case, information from the surface topography is suppressed allowing the relationship between the number of backscattered electrons produced and the atomic number of the sample to provide the contrast in the image. Conversely, if the signals are *subtracted* then topographical information is the primary source of contrast.

The backscattered image made is also very useful in reducing the effect on the image of charging of certain specimens since if the surface is covered with an insulating layer the backscattered electrons emitted from below the surface will be unaffected by this layer.

4.8. Photographic recording

Having optimized the image to obtain the required information at the

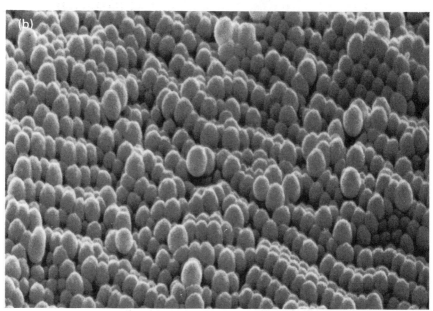

Fig. 37. Tilt correction may introduce artefacts. (a) The specimen is of latex spheres tilted at 45°. (b) Use of 'tilt correction' actually distorts the spheres and makes them appear as ellipsoids. (c) The low magnification uncorrected image of a grid is tilted to a nominal angle of 45°. (d) Tilt correction is very sensitive to the angle selected, as the three images show; left = 43.5°, centre = 45°, right = 47.5°. (e) If it is important to obtain an undistorted image it may be better to photograph the specimen untilted.

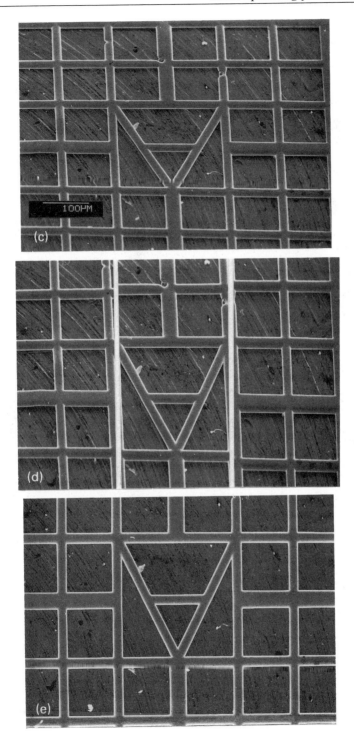

desired magnification and spot size the only variable left for photography is frame time. This has to be a compromise between noise reduction (requiring long times), drift, charging, and specimen damage, all of which require short times. Exposure times for special record CRTs (blue short persistence) are typically 60–100 s. This may be different if the viewing screen, which has a totally different long persistence phosphor, is being photographed. Brightness and contrast of the record CRT will have to be calibrated for the type of film and developer used.

All the instrumental variables discussed in the previous paragraphs can be optimized for one particular known sample in the microscope. To define the optimum conditions for an unknown sample begin by viewing it un-coated (coating may damage the surface) at the lowest possible accelerating voltage. The voltage should only be increased and/or the surface coated when it is clear that vital information is not being obscured.

5 TEM alignment procedures

Since the electron microscope is a multi-lens system, it will be necessary to align the instrument. In many modern instruments, certain lenses are sufficiently prealigned that they need no further adjustment by the operator, unless the microscope has been dismantled for cleaning when a complete alignment schedule will be necessary. However, since it is necessary to change the filament or the accelerating voltage quite frequently, some routine alignments will be necessary and are outlined in this chapter. The purpose of the alignment procedure is to ensure that the brightest image is obtained from the illumination system, that as the magnification is varied the same field of view remains on the screen, and that when the image is focused there is no lateral shift of the image. Finally, wherever possible the aberrations are corrected to allow maximum possible resolution from the sample. Each microscope manufacturer has a different approach to alignment. Early microscopes such as the AEI series required the lenses to be moved with respect to each other to ensure that the electrons were 'on axis'. In the modern series of instruments many of the alignments are preset with compensating coils positioned at strategic points in the column to shift or tilt the beam as necessary for the fine adjustments. Again, each manufacturer recommends a different approach to aligning the instrument. Philips takes the user through a series of steps, each one presetting magnification and/or illumination to a required level to allow a certain adjustment to be made. Although it is easy to achieve alignment by this method, it does not help to develop an understanding of microscope operation. Other manufacturers tell the operator which controls to preset and which controls to adjust. As long as the principles of alignment are understood, any microscope can be aligned by whatever method is preferred. It is hoped that the following general procedures will give a clear guide to aligning any microscope, although at times they have to be specific to certain models. It will also be noted that different manufacturers have different names for the same controls, e.g. condenser 2 is called CONDENSER by JEOL and INTENSITY by Philips. A list of the most commonly used controls is given in the back cover flap which includes space for the terms used on the reader's instrument to be inserted. In the following text when control names are used they are given in capital letters and refer to the function rather than to any manufacturer's name for it. You are recommended to read this section with the back cover flap open.

5.1. Illumination system

This section is concerned with the adjustment of the gun with respect to the condenser lenses and the condenser lenses with respect to the objective lens. It is assumed that the filament has been centred in the Wehnelt cap and the first stage will be to centre the emitted electron beam to the condenser lens. In some older instruments e.g. the AEI series, it was normal to fix the position of the gun and to move the anode plate, but in the majority of microscopes it is now normal to fix the anode and move the gun. This can either be a mechanical adjustment of the gun or deflection of the beam by a series of coils positioned close to the anode. Before starting on the actual alignment it is necessary to mention other controls in the illumination system which will be required to assist in the alignment. The deflection coils used in normal operation of the microscope, situated above the specimen, will be used at all times to centre the beam unless otherwise stated. These are known as BEAM SHIFT controls. It will be necessary to adjust the current in the two condenser lenses. The first condenser, C1, frequently has four to six settings, with the lowest number referring to the largest spot size. The second condenser, C2, is used at all times to control the spread of illumination on the screen. If the magnification is sufficiently low, there will be an intense area of illumination on the screen at focus. As the C2 lens is defocused, either by under- or over-focus, the entire screen may be illuminated. (Fig. 16(c) and (d)). Unless otherwise stated, when it is required to defocus the illumination the condenser 2 lens should be *over*-focused, normally a clockwise movement of the potentiometer. This lens (C2) usually has a coarse and a fine control, but for any one C1 setting it should only be necessary to use the fine control to defocus the illumination once the coarse setting has been found.

5.1.1. Obtaining an image

Switch on the accelerating voltage at the required value. (If a voltage in excess of 120 kV is to be used, this must be achieved slowly, allowing each voltage setting to stabilize before increasing the value.)

(i) Select a low magnification, say 5000 ×, with no specimen in the microscope.

(ii) Check that CONDENSER 1 is set to a large spot, say position 2.

(iii) Check that BEAM SHIFT controls are near their mid-position.

(iv) Remove the objective aperture.

(v) Remove the diffraction (selected area) aperture.
Do not remove the condenser aperture since this may cause excessive X-radiation to be emitted.

(vi) Select normal size condenser aperture (JEOL 200 μm, Philips 150 μm).

(vii) Slowly increase the FILAMENT CURRENT until saturation occurs (see Section 1.3).

For a first estimate of this, watch the beam current meter until there is no change in beam current with change of filament current. If in any doubt as to where this exact setting occurs, always choose slight under-saturation, since over-saturation gives no increase of brightness but a very marked reduction in filament life. As described in Section 1.3 the brightness reaches a maximum at saturation provided the gun is aligned; if not there will be a brightness maximum and it will then decrease as saturation is reached (see Fig. 5). Also, as shown in Fig. 38, if the image of the filament is viewed on the fluorescent screen before saturation, there will be a series of spots surrounding the central maximum. If the gun is aligned these will be symmetrical, but not if it is misaligned (Fig. 38(b)). Both these effects suggest a method of alignment but working with the unsaturated beam is probably easier (top Fig. 38). Having saturated the filament there should be illumination on the screen (if there is not, see the next section).

(viii) Focus the illumination with CONDENSER 2 control.

(ix) Desaturate the filament until the multiple spots are observed.

(x) Adjust GUN TILTS until the image is symmetrical (Fig. 38(a)).

(xi) Slowly increase FILAMENT CURRENT until all structure disappears in the spot. If it is necessary to move the illumination, use the BEAM SHIFT controls.

5.1.2. No illumination on screen

Since as shown in Fig. 5 the brightness will decrease as the FILAMENT CURRENT is raised if the gun is misaligned, instead of watching the beam current meter when saturating the filament, view the fluorescent screen and slowly increase the FILAMENT CURRENT until some illumination is visible on the screen. Once this point has been found increase the FILAMENT CURRENT slightly and the illumination will decrease. Return it to maximum brightness by adjusting the GUN TILTS. Continue to increase the filament current, keeping maximum brightness with the GUN TILTS until the multiple spots described in the above section are seen. Continue from part (viii) of Section 5.1.1.

If no illumination is seen at any position of filament current, remove the condenser aperture. *Caution:* As soon as any illumination is observed, reinsert the aperture.

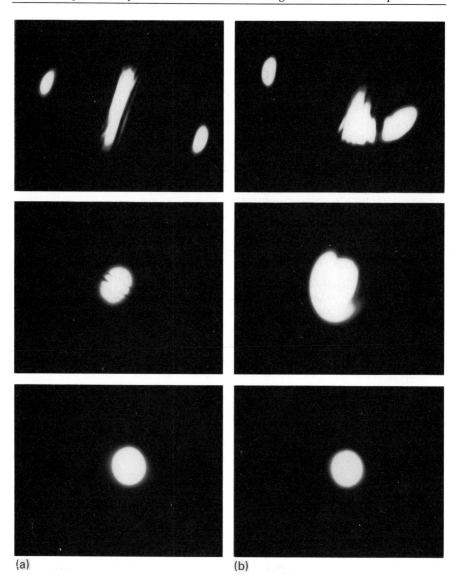

(a)   (b)

Fig. 38. The appearance of a fully focused beam when the gun is (a) aligned and (b) misaligned. In each case the filament is shown under-saturated (top), close to saturation (middle), and fully saturated (bottom). Compare these pictures with the saturation curve in Fig. 5.

5.1.3. Alignment of the gun to the condenser lenses

The alignment of the two condenser lenses is normally preset, but any misalignment of the gun is easily observed with variation of CONDENSER 1 control.

(i) Select a small spot, e.g. C1 on 4 or 5.
(ii) Focus the illumination with CONDENSER 2 control.
(iii) Centre with the BEAM SHIFT controls.
(iv) Change to largest spot (C1 on 1) and refocus the illumination. If the gun is misaligned the illumination will have moved.
(v) Return the spot to the centre with the GUN SHIFT alignment controls.

Repeat the above sequence until there is no movement of illumination with change of spot size (C1). If large adjustments were necessary it is advisable to re-check GUN TILT (Section 5.1.1).

5.2. Alignment of the condenser aperture

If the condenser aperture is misaligned, as CONDENSER 2 is varied from over- to under-focus the illumination will move across the screen (Figs 39 and 40). To align the aperture proceed as follows.

(i) Focus the illumination to a small spot with CONDENSER 2 control.
(ii) Centre with the BEAM SHIFT controls.
(iii) Defocus CONDENSER 2 until the illumination almost covers the screen.
(iv) Return the illumination to the centre with the X, Y condenser aperture controls.
(v) Refocus C2 and recentre the illumination using BEAM SHIFT.

Repeat this sequence until the spot expands and contracts about the screen centre as CONDENSER 2 is turned through focus.

5.3. Condenser astigmatism

As discussed in Section 1.5.3, if the condenser system is astigmatic instead of a circular spot on the screen there will be an ellipse (assuming the screen is flat!) with the major axis changing through 90° as CONDENSER 2 is changed from under- to over-focus.

If the stigmator is of the $r\theta$ type it is possible to follow a series of logical steps to correct astigmatism:

(i) Focus the illumination with CONDENSER 2 and centre it with BEAM SHIFT controls.
(ii) Set AMPLITUDE to zero and adjust CONDENSER 2 to obtain an ellipse (Fig. 41(a)). This is the inherent astigmatism in the microscope.
(iii) Increase AMPLITUDE to its maximum value (Fig. 41(b)). The major axis of the ellipse will almost certainly change direction.

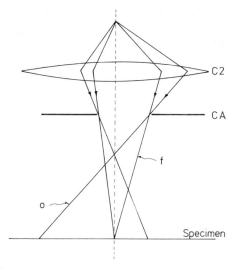

Fig. 39. The effect of a misaligned condenser aperture. The illumination can be focused with C2 and centred on the optical axis (rays f) but when the beam is spread by over-focusing C2 (rays o) the illumination is no longer concentric about the optical axis.

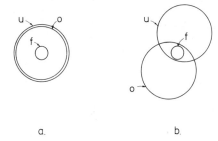

a.   b.

Fig. 40. The position of the illumination spot as C2 is changed from under-focused (u) through focus (f) to over-focused (o) when the condenser aperture is (a) aligned and (b) misaligned.

(iv) With ORIENTATION rotate the ellipse until the major axis is now perpendicular to the zero amplitude position (Fig. 41(c)).

(v) Now reduce AMPLITUDE until a circular spot is obtained (Fig. 41(d)).

It is important not to change CONDENSER 2 during this process since a change in condenser lens setting will change the orientation of the astigmatic image. If the stigmator is of the *(xy)* type it is easy to use both *x* and *y* controls to obtain a circular spot without following any logical sequence.

The alignments already discussed ensure that maximum illumination is available at high magnifications. Any misalignment will mean that it will be necessary to defocus CONDENSER 2 more to obtain even illumination.

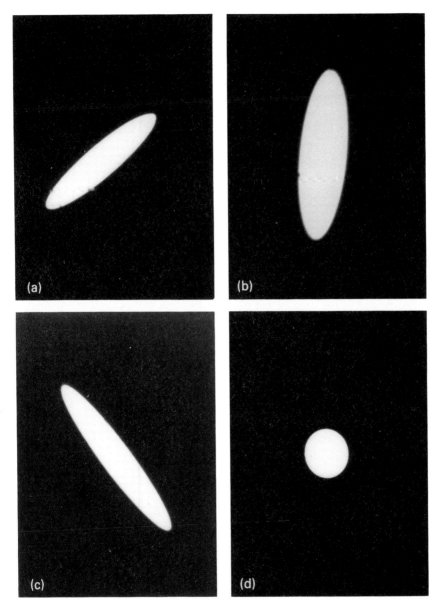

Fig. 41. The stages in the correction of condenser astigmatism as described in the text.

5.4. Alignment of the illumination with respect to the objective lens

Before commencing this stage of alignment a specimen must be introduced into the microscope. A suitable specimen is a perforated thin carbon film.

There are also additional controls to use. These often have a common name e.g. FOCUS refers to the focus of the objective lens on all microscopes, the only difference being that JEOL uses a series of controls ranging from coarse to fine whereas Philips uses one control to determine the focus step and the other control to focus. The MAGNIFICATION control will change more than one of the imaging lenses, as discussed in Section 1.10.1, but this is generally outside the operator's control.

Differences do arise in the names of the remaining imaging lenses. One that is frequently used is the lens to focus the diffraction pattern. This is required when, instead of normal imaging, the operator wants to 'look' at the back focal plane of the objective (Figs 23 and 24). Controls to ensure that the diffraction pattern is in focus on the screen (Fig. 24(b)) are called SA/HD DIFFRACTION CAMERA LENGTH on JEOL instruments and DIFFRACTION FOCUS on Philips microscopes.

If there is any misalignment in the objective lens, there will be a lateral translation of the image instead of just a rotation, when the image is focused. This will be explained with the help of Fig. 42. The ray diagram in Fig. 42(a) shows an object illuminated with parallel illumination. The object AA′ is imaged at BB′ (the object plane of the first projector lens). If the lens is defocused the new image plane will be CC′, but since the projector is 'looking' at BB′ it will see an out of focus image BB″, in the same position but in this case slightly larger. If the specimen is viewed with tilted illumination (Fig. 42(b)) there will be no change at focus, but when defocused, the

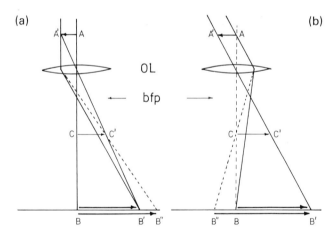

Fig. 42. The effect of tilted illumination (i.e. electrons not travelling parallel to the optical axis because of misalignment of the beam tilts): (a) when the system is aligned correctly a change in focus results in the image blurring (e.g. BB′ becomes BB″) and rotating about the optical axis (not shown in the diagram); (b) when the system is misaligned a change in focus results in the image at the centre of the screen shifting sideways (B to B″) as well as rotating about a point away from the optical axis.

projected image B″B′ will show a lateral shift. Therefore if there is no shift of the image with change of FOCUS then the instrument is aligned.

5.4.1. Alignment sequence for the objective lens

(i)   FOCUS image at a magnification of 10 000 ×.
(ii) With STAGE CONTROLS centre a small recognizable feature at the screen centre.
(iii) Focus and centre the illumination using the CONDENSER 2 and BEAM SHIFT.
(iv) Overfocus the illumination until the screen is evenly illuminated (There may be some interaction between tilt and shift controls and the effect will be minimized by spreading the beam).
(v)   Defocus the image by several medium FOCUS positions.
(vi) If the image moves return it to its former position using the BEAM TILT controls.
(vii) Repeat this sequence until no image movement is visible.
(viii) Repeat at a higher magnification (about 10 × higher).

In some microscopes there is an image wobbler which automatically varies the objective focus. When this is fitted start as before, but instead of defocusing, use the wobbler and adjust BEAM TILT until there is no image movement. Switch off the wobbler, recentre the illumination, and repeat.

5.4.2. Correction of tilt/shift compensation

If whilst correcting the illumination tilt excessive shift of the beam was observed, this is a result of the tilt being a combination of tilt and shift (Fig. 43) i.e. the tilt is not pivoted about the objective axis. In the JEOL series of microscopes there are two pairs of compensation coils to correct for this, one pair for the X direction and the other for the Y. The following procedure is adopted to adjust these.

(i)   Select 5000 × magnification.
(ii) Focus illumination with C2 and centre using BEAM SHIFTS.
(iii) Set X and Y BEAM TILTS to mid-position, i.e. zero tilt.
(iv) 'Rock' X BEAM TILT about centre value, if there is a shift of illumination, correct first the X, then the Y of the compensation coils until there is no illumination shift.
(v)   Repeat for the Y BEAM TILT, this time starting with the Y compensation.

For instruments such as the Philips 400T, the focus wobbler is used. Start as steps (i) and (ii) for JEOL instruments, and then proceed as follows.
(iii) Depress WOBBLER control and an elongated beam will be observed.

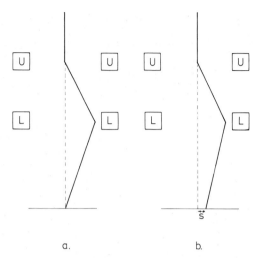

Fig. 43. (a) When the upper and lower tilt coils are compensated correctly tilt of the beam about a point on the specimen occurs. (b) With incorrect compensation tilt of the beam leads to a shift S as well.

> If correctly set it will appear as in Fig. 44(a), if not it will appear as Fig. 44(b).

(iv) Use the *X* BEAM TILT to obtain beam as in Fig. 44(a).

(v) Repeat in *Y* direction.

5.5. Centring the objective aperture

The final stages of routine alignment are the introduction of an objective aperture and the correction of the objective astigmatism. As mentioned in Section 1.9, the objective aperture is positioned in the back focal plane of the lens and as stated earlier in this section this plane can be examined by selecting DIFFRACTION. In order to view a sharp image of the diffraction pattern it will be necessary to insert a SELECTED AREA APERTURE.

(i) Select 1000 × magnification.

(ii) Defocus the illumination to cover screen (using C2).

(iii) FOCUS image.

(iv) Insert SELECTED AREA APERTURE and centre with aperture *X* and *Y* controls.

(v) Select DIFFRACTION mode.

(vi) Focus diffraction pattern with INTERMEDIATE LENS.

(vii) Insert OBJECTIVE APERTURE and centre with *X* and *Y* aperture controls about the centre of the diffraction pattern (Fig. 45).

(viii) Reselect MAGNIFICATION.

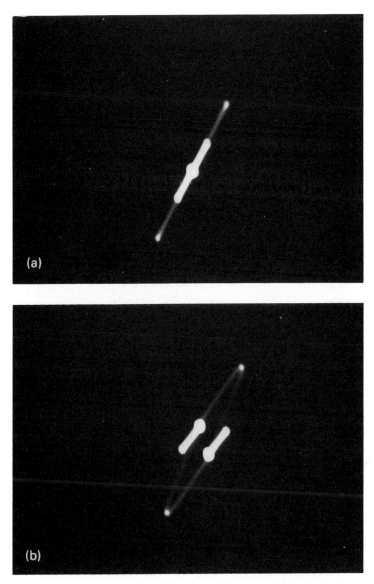

Fig. 44. Alignment of the tilt compensators using the wobbler on the Philips 400T: (a) aligned; (b) misaligned.

5.6. Correction of objective astigmatism

This is probably the most critical and most difficult correction. It necessitates viewing a high magnification image with the aid of the binoculars, and

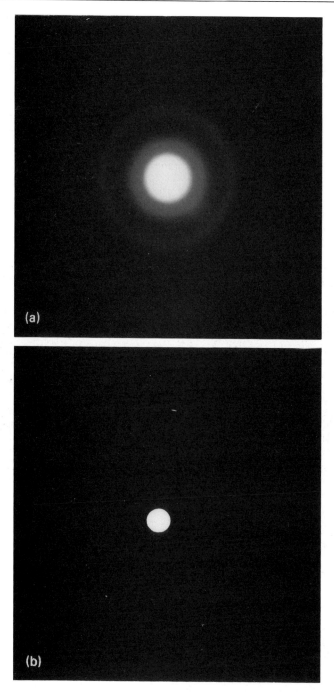

Fig. 45. The appearance of a diffraction pattern (a) before and (b) after the insertion of an objective aperture.

observing very fine structures at high magnifications (say 100 000 ×). A hole in a perforated carbon film test specimen, which may be coated with gold to increase contrast, is used and fringes are observed inside each hole as the objective lens is taken through focus. In the under-focused condition they will be light, and when over-focused they will be dark (Fig. 46). Focus is defined as the absence of a Fresnel fringe. These fringes arise from interference between scattered electrons at the edge of the carbon film and unscattered electrons (Fig. 47). At focus there will be no fringe, but if we defocus by an amount z then we can observe this interference effect. If the electron waves are in phase the beams will reinforce and the fringes will appear light; conversely, if they are out of phase they will interfere destructively and the fringe will appear dark.

The relationship between fringe width and defocus is $y^2/\lambda = z$, where y is the fringe width, λ is the electron wavelength and z is the defocus. The

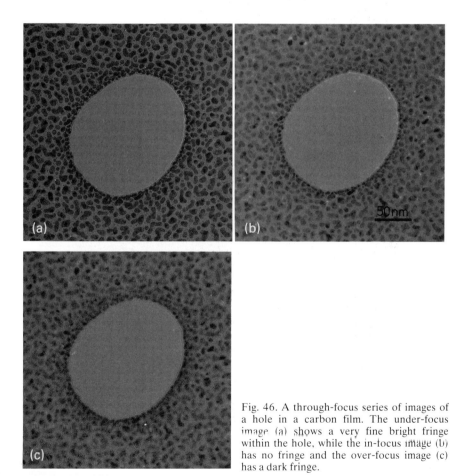

Fig. 46. A through-focus series of images of a hole in a carbon film. The under-focus image (a) shows a very fine bright fringe within the hole, while the in-focus image (b) has no fringe and the over-focus image (c) has a dark fringe.

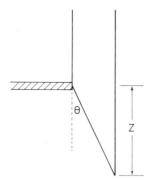

Fig. 47. The geometry of Fresnel diffraction at the edge of a specimen.

value of z corresponds to the focal setting of the focus controls e.g. ten 100 nm focus steps would mean a defocus of 1 μm giving a fringe width at 100 kV of approximately 6 nm.

If the image of a hole in the carbon film is astigmatic it is possible to observe the two astigmatic foci, seen as both light and dark fringes. Figures 48 and 49 shows the astigmatic image compared to the corrected image. If astigmatism is not to limit the resolution of the image then,

$$y_{max}^2 - y_{min}^2 \leqslant 1.4d^2$$

where d is the resolution and y_{max} and y_{min} are the widths of the biggest and smallest over-focused fringes around the inside of the hole.

To correct astigmatism an overfocused (dark) fringe very close to focus is viewed. If the procedure is not carried out very close to focus it may not be possible to observe the difference between the largest and smallest astigmatic fringes. For example, to correct the astigmatism to give 1 nm resolution then a value of $d = 1$ nm should be used in the above equation. Then if not working very close to focus y_{min} could be 2 nm and y_{max} would only be 2.3 nm. This means that we have to look for a difference between a 2 nm and a 2.3 nm fringe. However, by working closer to focus, so that $y_{min} = 0$ and $y_{max} = 1.2$ nm it is much easier to detect the differences between no fringe and a 1.2 nm fringe.

Hence, the following procedure is adopted to correct astigmatism.

(i) Select at least 100 000 × magnification, FOCUS the image, centre the beam to give uniform defocused illumination of reasonable screen brightness.

(ii) Observe a hole and adjust the FOCUS so that the fringe disappears round part of the hole with AMPLITUDE at zero if the *(rθ)* type of corrector is being used (Fig. 49(a)).

(iii) Increase AMPLITUDE to swamp the zero value (Fig. 49(b)).

(iv) With ROTATION orientate until the fringes are perpendicular to their zero value (Fig. 49(c)).

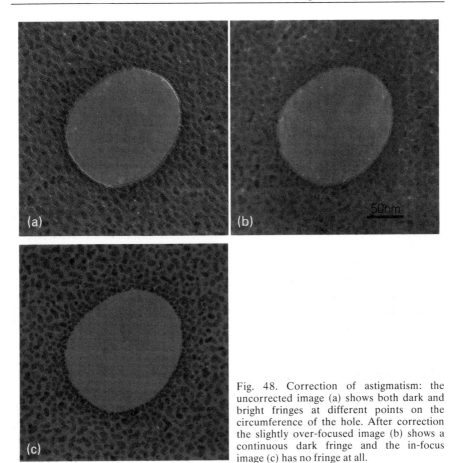

Fig. 48. Correction of astigmatism: the uncorrected image (a) shows both dark and bright fringes at different points on the circumference of the hole. After correction the slightly over-focused image (b) shows a continuous dark fringe and the in-focus image (c) has no fringe at all.

(v) Reduce AMPLITUDE to give a uniform fringe keeping very close to focus (Fig. 49(d)).

If the type of corrector is *(xy)* then it is easy to make adjustments *always keeping close to focus* until astigmatism has been corrected.

It is not always possible to perform the correction on a separate carbon film since the specimen may well modify the instrument's astigmatism. It can be seen that the background phase contrast image in Fig. 49 changed through 90° as focus was changed because the image astigmatism was uncorrected. This detail would just expand in size if the astigmatism were corrected. This can therefore be used as a method of correction. Simply focus the image such that detail is just visible then use the astigmatism controls as a fine focus. It can also be noticed that when the image was focused this was at minimum contrast. How sharp this minimum contrast is with focus depends on how well corrected the image was. In Fig. 50 it can

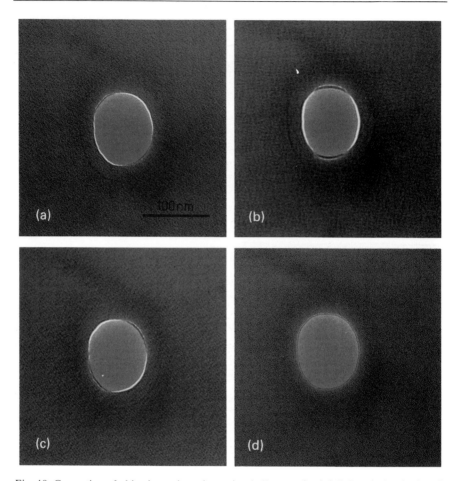

Fig. 49. Correction of objective astigmatism using $(r\theta)$ controls. A full description is given in the text.

be seen that contrast varies with correction. The following procedure is adopted to use this for trimming the previous correction.

(i)   Select image (minimum magnification 200 000 ×) and FOCUS.

(ii) Centre and defocus illumination (using C2).

(iii) Defocus the image, noting the number of objective FOCUS positions needed before any change in contrast is observed.

(iv) ReFOCUS image.

(v)   Adjust stigmator controls for minimum contrast.

(vi) Again check the defocus; the number of steps should have reduced.

(vii) Repeat this until you are satisfied that the sharpest contrast dip has been achieved.

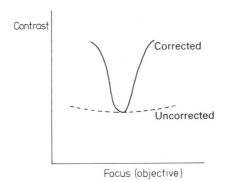

Fig. 50. The minimum contrast principle of astigmatism correction.

5.7. Alignment of intermediate lens

This correction can either be by mechanical movement of the pole piece (JEOL) or by deflection coils (Philips). When centring the objective aperture, it was possible that the diffraction pattern was not at the screen centre. This did not matter at that time since the aperture was centred about the diffraction centre. When taking photographs of diffraction patterns, however, it is obviously an advantage to have them at the screen centre. To correct on the JEOL move the intermediate lens ALIGN/3. On the Philips use the DIFFRACTION POINT ALIGNMENT. It may be necessary to repeat this for each camera length setting.

6 TEM operating procedures

It is fairly common practice, certainly when first introduced to an electron microscope, to find a set of conditions which give an image and to stay with these instead of optimizing the performance for each specimen. The following section should help you to select the working conditions which will optimize performance for a given specimen.

6.1. The gun

6.1.1. Accelerating voltage

Most modern microscopes have a wide kV range, say from 40–120 kV. At the high accelerating voltages there are more electrons of greater energy and shorter wavelength. This generally leads to a brighter image, greater penetration of the specimen, and higher resolution but lower amplitude contrast. The compromise setting for biological specimens is usually 80 kV where there is sufficient penetration and since biological samples are inherently low in contrast the improved microscope contrast is an advantage. However, if a very lightly stained (or even unstained) specimen is being used, there may well be an advantage in reducing the kV to 60 or even 40 kV, providing the specimen is not too thick. The improved contrast will far outweigh the marginal loss of resolution, particularly at the lower magnifications. Of course, if specimen penetation or resolution are of prime importance, it will be necessary to operate at the highest possible accelerating voltage. As far as the instrument is concerned, the higher the kV the more attention has to be given to maintenance and general cleanliness of the microscope, particularly the gun chamber, since at high kV gun instability will rapidly develop in a poor vacuum and in the presence of particulate material such as dust.

6.1.2. Bias

The beam current of the gun may be varied by the bias control. By increasing the bias setting more electrons are emitted but at the cost of filament life. It is therefore advisable to use high bias settings for minimum periods only.

6.2. Illumination system

Since the second condenser, C2, is used to 'spread' the beam the only two variables are spot size, C1, and condenser aperture.

6.2.1. Condenser aperture

As was shown in Chapter 1, the condenser aperture only limits the angular aperture of the illumination α_c when condenser 2 is fully focused (Fig. 21(a)); the aperture angle is then defined by the physical size of the aperture. A smaller angular aperture may be obtained by defocusing condenser 2, as shown in Fig. 21(b)). In general a large aperture is used to give a large number of electrons and hence a bright image over a larger area of the specimen.

If resolution is of prime importance a smaller angular aperture is required. This effect is readily observed by viewing a high magnification Fresnel fringe in a perforated carbon film. At focus of condenser 2, i.e. large α_c, the fringe will be unclear. As soon as condenser 2 is defocused, i.e. small α_c, the image will become considerably sharper. Also if beam damage is important the lower the number of electrons per unit area at the specimen the smaller the damage. The above implies that it is only necessary to operate with a large condenser aperture and defocus condenser 2. However, to avoid the risk of accidentally flooding the specimen with electrons as condenser 2 is focused it is better to work with a small physical condenser aperture when small α_c is required. This ensures that the maximum electron current reaching the specimen remains small even when condenser 2 is fully focused.

6.2.2. Spot size

The same considerations operate for spot size as for condenser aperture. With a large spot size (condenser 1) a greater area is illuminated at high current density but specimen damage is increased and resolution impaired. It is therefore essential to work with small spot size for high resolution imaging.

6.3. Objective aperture

The presence of an objective aperture is essential for virtually all contrast mechanisms to operate in the microscope. As the electrons interact with the specimen they are scattered over an angular range depending on mass and density. If there were no objective aperture most of the electrons would recombine with the unscattered electrons and form a featureless image. (There would be some contrast due to loss at fixed apertures etc.) If an objective aperture is introduced many of the scattered electrons will be stopped by the aperture and hence there will be fewer electrons in parts of the image with high mass and/or density and these regions will appear darker. This is shown in a very simplified schematic diagram (Fig. 2).

Therefore for high contrast a small objective aperture is normally required. However, other factors must be taken into consideration. The size of the objective aperture determines the ultimate resolution (in an ideal specimen). There are three major effects which act to limit resolution: these are diffraction, spherical, and chromatic aberrations (see Section 1.5). Spherical aberration increases as α_0^3, diffraction as $1/\alpha_0$ and chromatic aberration as α_0, where α_0 is the objective angular aperture, defined for the objective in the same way as the condenser aperture α_c in Fig. 21(a). Normally a compromise value of α_0 is chosen which gives a balance between the spherical aberration and diffraction effects, and this is the recommended aperture size assuming that there is negligible energy loss in the sample (i.e. if the sample is thin and chromatic aberrations can be ignored). However, for a thick sample this energy loss becomes significant and a small objective aperture will give better resolution.

There are special considerations if one is trying to image using phase contrast (e.g. a lattice image). The objective aperture must then be sufficiently large to allow the diffracted beam and the undeviated beam to interfere. Thus the aperture must pass electrons at an angle θ from the undeviated beam in order to image a fine structure of spacing d. θ is related to d via $\theta = \lambda/d$ and therefore, for a lens focal length f_0, the diameter D of the objective aperture is given by

$$D = 2f_0\lambda/d.$$

As an example, in order to image the graphite lattice ($d = 0.34$ nm) at 100 kV ($\lambda = 0.0037$ nm) with a typical objective lens ($f_0 = 2$ mm), a 50 μm aperture would be required (since $D = 43.5$ μm). It should also be noted that for a thin phase object such as a very thin carbon film the contrast is not improved by insertion of the objective aperture.

6.4. Focusing

Focusing the image can be difficult in the electron microscope, particularly at low magnifications. At higher magnification it becomes easier since the in-focus image will show the least contrast. Fine detail will be enhanced by phase contrast on each side of focus.

At lower magnification, with an objective aperture inserted, true focus is far from obvious, and manufacturers supply a focus wobbler. This wobbler acts by rapidly tilting the illumination at the specimen plane. If the image is in focus there will be no image movement but if it is out of focus there will be lateral movement of the image (compare with Fig. 42 showing correction of tilt of the illumination system). Low magnification images are best taken at focus since defocusing will result in a granular appearance. At higher magnifications it can be an advantage to enhance certain regular spacings (e.g. cell membranes, lattice images) but it must be remembered that although defocusing enhances certain spacings it will also reduce the visibility of others for the same defocus. Although it is possible to calculate the amount of defocus required (assuming that the focal length, spherical aberration and defocus step are known), in practice it is very easy to take a through-focal series of micrographs and subsequently select the under-focused image which improves the contrast of the desired feature.

6.5. Selection of magnification

6.5.1. Normal magnification range

Many users new to electron microscopy tend to take micrographs at a higher magnification than is necessary. As long as the detail is larger than the grain of the photographic image (see Section 6.6) the magnification should be kept to a minimum. Probably the main reason for overmagnification is the relatively poor image resolved on the fluorescent screen. The photographic film will resolve at least a factor of five better than the screen and with greatly improved contrast. There is certainly no problem in magnifying the film five times and since the image will be brighter and require less exposure at lower magnifications the resultant photograph will be superior due to reduced beam damage and specimen drift.

6.5.2. Low magnification imaging

As described in Section 1.10.1, at low magnification the objective lens is either switched off or weakened to obtain a very low magnification image (about $100 \times$). It is therefore necessary to remove the objective aperture since this is no longer at the back focal plane and will limit the field of view. This will have two noticeable effects on the image; contrast will be reduced and the charge distribution on the specimen will be altered possibly causing charging and disruption of the specimen. The second problem can be overcome by coating the specimen with a thin carbon film. It is obviously an advantage to be able to photograph the specimen at a magnification less than $1000 \times$ since correlation with light microscopy is then feasible. More importantly this allows the relationship between the actual area photographed at high magnification and the whole specimen to be recorded. The loss of contrast mentioned above can be overcome by using a diffraction aperture as the contrast aperture. Since this will not be at the back focal plane of the intermediate lens it will be necessary to select the largest aperture so as not to limit the field of view. Focusing can be difficult at these very low magnifications since the wobbler is not always operational in this range. If this is the case focus can be obtained either by removing the diffraction aperture and focusing for minimum contrast or by reducing the depth of focus by focusing condenser 2.

6.6. Photographic recording

To take a photograph in the electron microscope is usually very simple since it is only necessary to raise the screen and allow the electron image to fall directly on to the photographic emulsion, which nowadays is normally cut film. Probably because it is so easy little attention is paid to the process, but to obtain the best results some understanding of the exposure of a photographic emulsion is necessary.

6.6.1. Grain

Graininess in a normal photographic image is taken to be the size of the developed silver halide grains, usually about 1 μm. In the electron micrograph this is unlikely to be the case. The grain in this image is due to the random arrival of electrons on the film and this 'noise' in the electron micrograph is an order of magnitude larger than photographic grain, i.e. 10 μm. The speed of the emulsion will alter the grain size in a similar manner to light exposure so for a fast emulsion the image will be 'grainier' not due to grain size but due to the smaller number of electrons required to expose the emulsion and hence the greater random noise.

6.6.2. Contrast

Again there is a different process involved. A single electron renders a silver halide grain fully developable unlike exposure to light where several tens of photons are required. The outcome of this is that contrast becomes directly proportional to the optical density of the emulsion, therefore any emulsion exposed and developed to the same density will have the same contrast. To vary the contrast it is necessary to vary the density. Thus in order to photograph a specimen which shows rather weak contrast either a longer exposure time should be used or the negative over-developed. There is of course a limit to this as the emulsion will eventually become saturated, but in the normal photographic density range up to $d = 1.5$ it will hold true. (A density of 1 means that 10% of light is transmitted through the film.)

6.6.3. Choice of emulsion

This is somewhat limited by what is obtainable from photographic suppliers. The major suppliers make special electron microscope emulsions, one of the main requirements being a very uniform thickness since any variation in thickness will result in uneven exposure. Although the major consideration is the response to electrons the film must also be exposed by light since information such as magnification, accelerating voltage, and film number are usually also recorded on the film.

6.6.4. Photography in the microscope

Exposure in modern instruments is usually automatic. The screen is used to measure the number of electrons arriving and the exposure time required is calculated and displayed. This does assume a fairly uniform image, but if a grid bar occupies a fair proportion of the screen the actual region of interest will be overexposed. In the Philips 400T, for example, it is possible to insert a small screen and use this for setting the exposure on a local area of the specimen. If this is not possible a correction must be made. There is normally a preset control which is used in the initial calibration of the system. This should not be considered as a preset control but as a density and hence contrast control. If the image is low in contrast, then the film should be exposed to a greater density. Also the calibration will be made at the most commonly used accelerating voltage and, although it will hold over a limited kV range, the response of the film varies with accelerating voltage and thus a density correction will have to be made at extremes of kV. The length of exposure is a compromise between a well defocused illumination and specimen drift, and should normally be kept to only a few seconds.

6.6.5. Uneveness of the developed film

There could be several causes of uneven density of the exposed film. The most likely are listed below.
  (i) Inadequate agitation during development of the film.
 (ii) Insufficient defocus of condenser 2 so that the centre of the micrograph has greater exposure.
(iii) At low magnification any distortion of the image will mean that the magnification at the centre will be different from that at the edge and hence the intensity will vary.
 (vi) Uneven emulsion.

6.6.6. Printing TEM negatives

When printing elecron micrographs it is recommended to use an opal lamp with a good condenser system as this will give a crisper image with greater contrast than the cold cathode system often found in multi-user darkrooms.

6.7. Drift

Unless there is a fault, drift of the image is unlikely to occur as a result of movement of the TEM stage, although a dirty specimen holder will make poor contact and hence encourage drift. The specimen itself can cause problems. These could arise from poor adhesion of the film to the support grid, a broken film adjacent to the area being viewed, a large particle causing localised heating, and a non-conducting specimen may charge slightly. Most of these effects will become more noticeable as condenser 2 is changed. After focusing the image, the subsequent defocus of condenser 2 changes the charge distribution and hence the specimen may drift. It is advisable to allow the specimen and holder to stabilize at the working microscope temperature as this may be different from room temperature. The result of a small amount of specimen drift will be a streaking of fine structure in the image. This can be distinguished from astigmatism by taking a through-focus series; if drift is present the direction of smearing will not change but if astigmatism is responsible the direction of the smearing will change by 90° on either side of focus. Drift rate is easily measured by double exposure of an image over a known time interval and measuring the distance moved. A more immediate method is to examine the region of interest through the binoculars. It should not move for a period of ten times the required exposure.

7 Scanning techniques in the TEM

With the addition of a scanning module to the transmission electron micro-scope the range of possible techniques is greatly extended. These units allow the beam to be scanned across an area of the specimen and with the addition of suitable detectors the microscope can be used in a surface imaging mode (SEM) or in a scanned transmission mode (STEM). Figure 51 shows how the Philips EM 400T is operated in the scanning modes.

7.1. SEM

The SEM detector looks at electrons which have been scattered from the specimen surface. In addition to the electron beam interactions described in Chapter 1 (Fig. 2), many electrons carrying very low energies are emitted from both surfaces of a thin specimen, as shown in Fig. 52. These are generally called secondary electrons and enable us to use the microscope as an SEM (scanning electron microscope). Other electrons will be back-scattered without appreciable loss of energy. These are called back-scattered or reflected electrons and lead to another possible imaging mode.

In Fig. 51 the positions of the detectors for SEM are shown. The second-ary detector, for low energy electrons, is normally a scintillator and light guide coupled to a photo-multiplier, as on a conventional SEM. The back-scattered detector, for high energy electrons, is usually a solid state device and is more useful for obtaining information about specimen composition since the number of backscattered electrons depends quite strongly on the atomic number of the specimen. The main advantage of having SEM avail-able on a TEM (apart from just using it as a high resolution SEM for looking at solid surfaces) is to be able to view the surface of a thin speci-men. It is often advantageous to compare SEM and TEM images in order to find out whether the surface is flat (which it usually is not) or to determine if the area of interest, particularly during analysis, is on the top or bottom surface of the support film. If a particle is on the lower surface there may be a reduction in count rate of low energy X-rays since they will be absorbed in the support film.

7.2. STEM

Figure 51 shows the comparison between the TEM and STEM imaging systems. In the TEM imaging mode the image is magnified by the projector

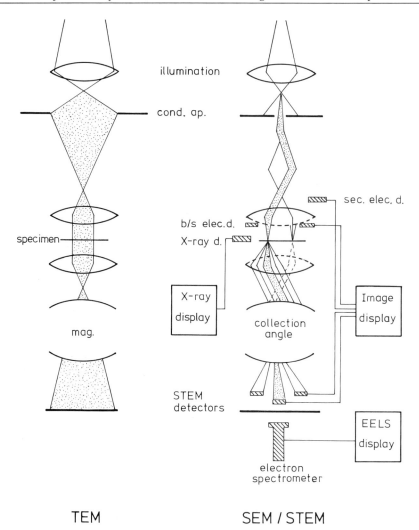

TEM   SEM / STEM

Fig. 51. A comparison of the ray paths in TEM and SEM/STEM for the Philips EM 400T. The usual positions of all the detectors mentioned in the text are indicated on the SEM/STEM diagram.

lenses and displayed on the fluorescent screen, whereas the STEM image is set up in the (TEM) diffraction mode and the projector lenses are used only to vary the collection angle. The STEM detector is thus effectively in an equivalent position to the back focal plane of the objective lens so that the central (undeflected) electrons are collected on the bright field detector and the deflected (scattered or diffracted) electrons fall on the dark field detector. The resultant bright field STEM image is similar in appearance to the normal TEM image, as long as the convergence angle and aperture sizes

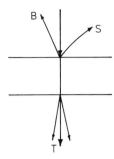

Fig. 52. The three major types of electron emitted from a thin specimen are the transmitted (T), high energy backscattered (B), and the low energy secondary (S) electrons.

are equivalent. However, there are advantages to working in the STEM mode.

As with the SEM, the STEM image is magnified and displayed on a cathode ray tube (CRT). Magnification is now determined by the ratio of the size of the area scanned to the size of the CRT. The contrast can be controlled electronically by manipulating the signal from the photomultiplier. This means that a specimen with intrinsically low contrast, such as an unstained biological section, can be viewed with reasonable contrast in the image. Also, because the imaging technique involves no lenses below the specimen, chromatic aberrations are reduced.

In both scanning modes (SEM and STEM) the spot size must be much smaller than that usually needed in TEM, since the resolution is ultimately limited to the diameter of the beam. A minimum spot size of about 2.5 nm is now common on TEM/STEM instruments. This means that for X-ray analysis and microdiffraction it is possible to obtain information from a very small region of the specimen. This advantage is not so crucial on the Philips 400 series which can be operated in TEM in their 'nanoprobe' mode with a spot size as small as 4 nm. However, in all current instruments the STEM mode provides access to the very smallest spot sizes.

7.3. Alignment

There are major differences in philosophy between manufacturers concerning the position and use of STEM and SEM detectors and therefore detailed alignment procedures vary considerably among individual instruments. Philips microscopes have a retractable STEM detector above the fluorescent screen and use the TEM DIFFRACTION mode to set up the conditions for operation in STEM. On the other hand JEOL instruments have a fixed STEM detector located beneath the fluorescent screen (which must therefore be raised) and use the normal TEM MAGNIFICATION condition for setting up. However the common features for alignment are as follows.

(i) The TEM must be well aligned.

(ii) A set of alignment controls is supplied on the scanning attachment. This is to ensure that the beam is centred on switching to SCANNING.

(iii) TEM controls are often duplicated on the scanning attachment so that, in the SCANNING mode, focusing and spot size are controlled locally. The controls often carry the same names as the TEM controls, but sometimes operate on different lenses.

7.4. Diffraction

In conventional electron diffraction the region of interest is selected by means of a physical aperture (Section 1.10.2). The smallest area which can be selected by this technique is limited by the spherical aberration of the objective lens and is usually about 1 μm in diameter. By using the small probes obtainable either in 'nanoprobe' or scanning modes it is possible to select a smaller area of the specimen with the focused beam. This will give, depending on the convergence angle set by the condenser aperture, a micro-selected area diffraction pattern (Fig. 53(a)) or a convergent beam diffraction pattern (Fig. 53(b)).

7.5. Analysis

The two techniques of energy dispersive X-ray analysis (EDX) and electron

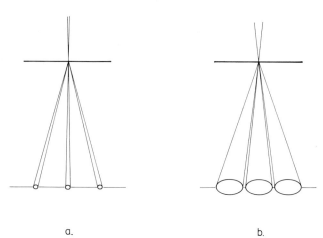

a.   b.

Fig. 53. The approximate geometry of (a) microdiffraction and (b) convergent beam diffraction. The only significant difference is in the beam convergence angle at the specimen.

energy loss analysis (EELS) are now frequently available on TEM/STEM instruments. The first uses characteristic X-rays excited from the small volume of specimen irradiated by the beam, while the second detects the energy lost by electrons which have interacted with the specimen. The EDS detector is fitted to the side of the microscope close to the specimen, whereas the EELS spectrometer sits beneath the fluorescent screen (Fig. 51). For both these types of analysis it is useful to be able to define the analysed region by focusing the beam on to a small area using either 'nanoprobe' or scanning modes.

Afterword

With this book open in front of you, and the individual labelling of your instrument filled in on the front or back flap, you should be able to align any working SEM or TEM. Although the text has been written with frequent reference to the most widely available series of microscopes in the UK, it is equally applicable to the alignment and operation of the many Zeiss, Hitachi, CAMSCAN, ISI and other instruments to be found around the world. The principles of EM operation are also unlikely to change radically in the future, although more of the functions which we now perform manually will undoubtedly come under microprocessor control. We therefore hope that this book will be useful for many years to come.

A final exhortation is necessary, particularly to those readers who are complete newcomers to electron microscopy. Microscopes are expensive but film is (relatively) cheap. You will only improve your skill as a microscopist by taking micrographs. We recommend that, from your second session at the microscope onwards, you expose large numbers of films. Process and examine each batch as you go and you will rapidly improve. If you sit at the microscope desk painstakingly trying to get everything perfect before you take a micrograph it may be weeks before you have a picture in your hands and your progress will be slow. Ignore all Jeremiahs who tell you that film is expensive; only by practice will you perfect your technique. Happy shooting!

Bibliography

In addition to the other RMS Handbooks, Goodhew and Humphreys (1988) provides a useful introduction to the 'why' (rather than 'how') of both scanning and transmission electron microscopy.

S. K. Chapman (1986). *Working with a scanning electron microscope.* Lodgemark Press.

A. M. Glauert (ed.) (1970–1988). *Practical methods in electron microscopy,* several volumes. Elsevier.

J. I. Goldstein, D. E. Newbury, P. Echlin, D. C. Joy, C. Fiori, and E. Lifshin (1981). *Scanning electron microscopy and X-ray microanalysis.* Plenum Press.

P. J. Goodhew and F. J. Humphreys (1988). *Electron microscopy and analysis.* Taylor & Francis (London).

J. J. Hren, J. I. Goldstein and D. C. Joy (eds) (1979). *Introduction to analytical electron microscopy.* Plenum Press.

G. Thomas and M. J. Goringe (1979). *Transmission electron microscopy of materials.* John Wiley.

RMS Handbooks 3, 8, and 16. (See details below.)

Peter J. Goodhew (1984). *Specimen preparation for transmission electron microscopy of materials.* Royal Microscopical Society Microscopy Handbooks, no. 3. Oxford University Press, Oxford.

S. K. Chapman (1986). *Maintaining and monitoring the transmission electron microscope.* Royal Microscopical Society Microscopy Handbooks, No. 8. Oxford University Press, Oxford.

P. M. Budd and Peter J. Goodhew (1988). *Light-element analysis in the transmission electron microscope: WEDX and EELS.* Royal Microscopical Society Microscopy Handbooks, No. 16. Oxford University Press, Oxford.

Many aspects of the operation of electron microscopes are illustrated in several microcomputer software packages which are available for BBC or IBM PC computers. These interactive animated graphics-based programs show changes in the electron-optical ray paths more clearly than can any single diagram in this book. The most relevant titles are:

The Scanning Electron Microscope, F. J. Humphreys, Institute of Metals Engineering Materials Software Series 409 (BBC) and 438 (IBM).

The Transmission Electron Microscope, P. J. Goodhew, Institute of Metals Engineering Materials Software Series 410 (BBC) and 437 (IBM).

These titles can be ordered from the Institute of Metals at 1 Carlton House Terrace, London SW1Y 5DB.

Index